2nd Workshop on Novel Incentives in Data Collection from People: Models, Implementations, Challenges and Results (NIDCP 2022)

Held at LREC 2022

Marseille, France
20 – 25 June 2022

Editors:

James Fiumara
Christopher Cieri
Mark Liberman
Chris Callison-Burch

ISBN: 978-1-7138-6129-4

Printed from e-media with permission by:

Curran Associates, Inc.
57 Morehouse Lane
Red Hook, NY 12571

Some format issues inherent in the e-media version may also appear in this print version.

Association for Computational Linguistics
209 N. Eighth Street
Stroudsburg, Pennsylvania 18360

Phone: 1-570-476-8006
Fax: 1-570-476-0860

acl@aclweb.org

Additional copies of this publication are available from:

Curran Associates, Inc.
57 Morehouse Lane
Red Hook, NY 12571 USA
Phone: 845-758-0400
Fax: 845-758-2633
Email: curran@proceedings.com
Web: www.proceedings.com

LREC 2022 Workshop
Language Resources and Evaluation Conference
20-25 June 2022

2nd Workshop on Novel Incentives in Data Collection from People: models, implementations, challenges and results (NIDCP 2022)

PROCEEDINGS

Editors:
James Fiumara, Christopher Cieri, Mark Liberman, Chris Callison-Burch

2nd Workshop on Novel Incentives in Data Collection from People: models, implementations, challenges and results (NIDCP 2022)

Edited by: James Fiumara, Christopher Cieri, Mark Liberman, Chris Callison-Burch

For more information:
European Language Resources Association (ELRA)
9 rue des Cordelières
75013, Paris
France
http://www.elra.info
Email: lrec@elda.org

Introduction

The many research communities that rely upon Language Resources (LR) have benefitted from massive contributions from data centers, government agencies and research groups around the world. Nevertheless, research potential remains largely untapped because the LRs that fuel development fall far short of need as measured by volume, data type, and language coverage. Searches for data sets regularly go unfulfilled even for the dozen languages with the greatest populations and gross linguistic products.

Notwithstanding advances in data collection and processing, the supply of LRs continues to lag behind need in part because of the limited incentive models employed. Throughout the history of LR development, the commonest incentives offered to people in exchange for their contributions of raw language data and judgements were monetary. Perhaps this tendency is based on convenience or perhaps it reflects a belief concerning the ethics of data contribution. In any case, that bias has limited the LR user communities' ability to collect data for example: in the absence of ready funding, in situations where funding cannot easily be transferred and, from groups, such as indigenous communities, with other motivations. The focus on monetary incentives has also limited opportunities to understand how other incentives might attract different workforces, what kinds of workflows might be optimal for such workforces and how their contributions could be integrated into research and technology development efforts.

Social media in contrast has employed a wider range of incentives including: access to information and entertainment; possibilities for self-expression, sharing and publicizing intellectual or creative work; chances to vent frustrations or convey thoughts sometimes anonymously; forums for socializing; situations in which to develop competence that may lead to new prospects; competition, status, prestige, and recognition; payment or discounts in real and virtual worlds; access to services and infrastructure based on contributions; opportunities to contribute to a greater cause or good.

Within HLT communities there have been a few projects that employ these incentives. SPICE provided contributors with access to a speech recognition system that was built from their own contributions. Let's Go improved access to public transit. Herme offered the unusual experience of interacting with a tiny, cute robot. Crowd Curio offered experiential learning of e.g. historical linguistic behaviors. "On Everyone's Mind and Lips" mapped the linguistic landscape of Austria. LanguageARC offers citizen linguists opportunities to contribute to research on timely issues such as bias in public discourse, documenting under-resourced languages and building normative models that can be used in the study of neuro-divergence and neurodegenerative disease.

However, outside our fields, and sometimes outside our reach, are efforts that employ variable incentives to a much greater effect creating massive LRs. LibriVox offer contributors the chance to create audio recordings of classic works of literature, develop their skills as reader and voice actors, work within a community of similarly minded volunteers and enable access to the blind, illiterate and others for whom existing versions were inaccessible. On the other hand, researchers cannot always rely on contributions from social media providers whose products are not always well matched to our research questions or who may be unable or unwilling to share their holdings in the ways that our research programs need.

Given the perpetual need for larger and more diverse LRs, the success of novel incentives in other fields that collect data from human contributors and the early successes and growth of interest among LR creators, this workshop will continue the discussion from the 2016 LREC Workshop on Novel Incentives in Data Collection and the 2020 LREC Workshop on Citizen Linguistics and Language Resource Development.

Organizers

Chris Callison-Burch, University of Pennsylvania (USA)
Christopher Cieri, Linguistic Data Consortium, University of Pennsylvania (USA)
James Fiumara, Linguistic Data Consortium, University of Pennsylvania (USA)
Mark Liberman, Linguistic Data Consortium, University of Pennsylvania (USA)

Program Committee:

Nicoletta Calzolari, CNR-ILC (Italy)
Jon Chamberlain, University of Essex (United Kingdom)
Yiya Chen, Leiden University (Netherlands)
Christopher Cieri, Linguistic Data Consortium, University of Pennsylvania (USA)
Maxine Eskenazi, Carnegie Mellon University (USA)
James Fiumara, Linguistic Data Consortium, University of Pennsylvania (USA)
Karën Fort, Sorbonne Université (France)
Bruno Guillaume, INRIA (France)
Matthew Lease, University of Texas at Austin (USA)
Mark Liberman, Linguistic Data Consortium, University of Pennsylvania (USA)
Massimo Poesio, Queen Mary University of London (United Kingdom)
Odette Scharenborg, Delft University of Technology (Netherlands)
Jennifer Tracey, Linguistic Data Consortium, University of Pennsylvania (USA)
Jonathan Wright, Linguistic Data Consortium, University of Pennsylvania (USA)
Jiahong Yuan, Baidu (China)

Table of Contents

Workshop Program

9:00–9:20	*The NIEUW Project: Developing Language Resources through Novel Incentives* James Fiumara, Christopher Cieri, Mark Liberman, Chris Callison-Burch, Jonathan Wright and Robert Parker
9:20–9:40	*Use of a Citizen Science Platform for the Creation of a Language Resource to Study Bias in Language Models for French: A Case Study* Karën Fort, Aurélie Névéol, Yoann Dupont and Julien Bezançon
9:40–10:00	*Fearless Steps APOLLO: Advanced Naturalistic Corpora Development* John H.L. Hansen, Aditya Joglekar, Szu-Jui Chen, Meena Chandra Shekar and Chelzy Belitz
10:00–10:20	*Creating Mexican Spanish Language Resources through the Social Service Program* Carlos Daniel Hernandez Mena and Ivan Vladimir Meza Ruiz
11:00–11:20	*Fictionary-Based Games for Language Resource Creation* Steinunn Rut Friðriksdóttir and Hafsteinn Einarsson
11:20–11:40	*Using Mixed Incentives to Document Xi'an Guanzhong* Juhong Zhan, Yue Jiang, Christopher Cieri, Mark Liberman, Jiahong Yuan, Yiya Chen and Odette Scharenborg
11:40–12:00	*Crowdsourced Participants' Accuracy at Identifying the Social Class of Speakers from South East England* Amanda Cole
12:00–12:20	*About the Applicability of Combining Implicit Crowdsourcing and Language Learning for the Collection of NLP Datasets* Verena Lyding, Lionel Nicolas and Alexander König
12:20–12:40	*The Influence of Intrinsic and Extrinsic Motivation on the Creation of Language Resources in a Citizen Linguistics Project about Lexicography* Barbara Heinisch

The NIEUW Project: Developing Language Resources Through Novel Incentives

James Fiumara, Christopher Cieri, Mark Liberman, Chris Callison-Burch*, Jonathan Wright, Robert Parker

University of Pennsylvania Linguistic Data Consortium and *Department of Computer and Information Science

{jfiumara, ccieri, myl, jdwright, parkerrl} @ldc.upenn.edu, {ccb} @cis.upenn.edu

Abstract

This paper provides an overview and update on the Linguistic Data Consortium's (LDC) NIEUW (Novel Incentives and Workflows) project supported by the National Science Foundation and part of LDC's larger goal of improving the cost, variety, scale, and quality of language resources available for education, research, and technology development. NIEUW leverages the power of novel incentives to elicit linguistic data and annotations from a wide variety of contributors including citizen scientists, game players, and language students and professionals. In order to align appropriate incentives with the various contributors, LDC has created three distinct web portals to bring together researchers and other language professionals with participants best suited to their project needs. These portals include LanguageARC designed for citizen scientists, Machina Pro Linguistica designed for students and language professionals, and LingoBoingo designed for game players. The design, interface, and underlying tools for each web portal were developed to appeal to the different incentives and motivations of their respective target audiences.

Keywords: novel incentives, citizen science, language resources

1. Introduction

Human language technologies (HLT), linguistic research, and language teaching all rely heavily on a variety of Language Resources (LRs) and have benefited immensely from decades of linguistic data creation and sharing supported by governments and research institutes. Continued efforts from data centers such as LDC[1], European Language Resources Association (ELRA)[2], LDC for Indian Languages[3], and South African Center for Digital Language Resources (SADiLaR)[4] have made large amounts of data available to the research community. However, the overall amount of LRs available globally still falls short of need. Traditional approaches are unlikely to meet the needs of the research community due to finite resources of funding versus the effort required to create these LRs. LDC's NIEUW projects seeks to close this gap by using novel incentives and workflows to collect linguistic data and judgments and to make these data available world-wide to the research community.

2. Novel Incentives and LR Creation

Given the high cost and extensive effort that goes into collecting and annotating linguistic resources, HLT researchers have increasingly looked to alternative incentive models and crowdsourcing options such as Amazon Mechanical Turk (MTurk). While MTurk's ability to collect large numbers of discrete HITs (Human Intelligent Tasks) at extremely low cost per HIT allows the creation of resources for as little as 1/10th the typical cost (Callison-Burch and Dredze 2010), the crowdsourcing platform is not without issues including variable annotation quality (Tratz and Hovy 2010) and, more importantly, ethical concerns of exploitive labor practices (Fort et al. 2011). MTurk is certainly one alternative to traditional linguistic resource creation practices in its utilization of large-scale crowdsourcing rather than employing a small group of experts, but ultimately the platform still relies on the incentive of monetary compensation, even if comparably small amounts of it meted out by microtask. However, even outside of ethical concerns, this reliance on monetary compensation is ineffective when there is a lack of funding, when monetary payment is not permitted, or when potential contributors are motivated by factors other than money and can be problematic when workers use unexpected means to maximize their earnings.

Alternatively, citizen science, social media, and games with a purpose (GWAP) have shown that people are willing to volunteer large amounts of time and effort given appropriate non-monetary incentives which can include entertainment, competition, learning and education, social interaction, demonstrating expertise, and contributing to a social good. Successful examples outside of the HLT community are many, including LibriVox[5] which organizes volunteers to record audiobooks from out-of-copyright works which are then made freely available to the public and Zooniverse[6], an online citizen science platform that has recruited over two million volunteers generating over six hundred million classifications for a variety of research projects in astronomy, zoology, biology, medicine, history, and climate science. Novel incentives have also been used effectively inside of the HLT community including the now defunct The Great Language Game (Skirgård, Roberts & Yencken 2017) which collected tens of millions of language identification judgments and Phrase Detectives, an online game with a purpose which has collected millions of judgments on anaphoric expressions in two languages since going live in 2008 (Poesio et al. 2016).

Building upon these models, the NIEUW project enhances LR development well beyond what project-dependent, direct funding alone can accomplish by creating an infrastructure that enables the ongoing construction of scalable data collection and annotation activities available

[1] https://www.ldc.upenn.edu

[2] http://www.elra.info

[3] https://www.ldcil.org

[4] https://sadilar.org

[5] https://librivox.org

[6] https://www.zooniverse.org

Proceedings of the 2nd Workshop on Novel Incentives in Data Collection from People @LREC2022, pages 1–7

to the public via the web and mobile devices and designed with appropriate incentive models in mind.

We argue that the best way to attract and engage non-traditional workforces is to offer a variety of incentives that are organized in separate, but not mutually exclusive, groupings. We have identified three already existing communities that we think present the most promise: 1) citizen scientists who are motivated to participate in linguistic research due to an interest in language and culture or the desire to contribute to research and technology development; 2) language students and professionals such as linguists, transcriptionists and professors who work directly with linguistic data but would benefit from improved tools and infrastructure; 3) game players who seek entertainment, challenge, and competition.

For NIEUW we have created three web portals geared towards each of these communities containing language collection and annotation activities and games designed to appeal to the respective groups. The website design, task size and complexity, tool builders and workflows were all created with the relevant participant populations in mind. Although LDC initially created tasks for these portals, they have since been made available to research collaborators. By allowing language researchers to create their own projects on these portals, the infrastructure not only serves the larger research community but creates a sustainable resource that can continue to grow without being tethered to any particular project goal or funding requirement.

3. LanguageARC : A Portal for Citizen Linguistics

Crowd-sourced contributions to scientific research by the general public (often called "citizen science") has a long history from Edmund Halley who solicited the public to help map solar eclipses (Pasachoff 1999) to bird lovers helping the Audubon Society count or track birds (Root 1988). Recent technologies such as the internet and smart phones have made it even easier for the public to contribute to science. Building on this history, LanguageARC[7] (**A**nalysis **R**esearch **C**ommunity) is a citizen science platform and community dedicated to language research ("citizen linguistics").

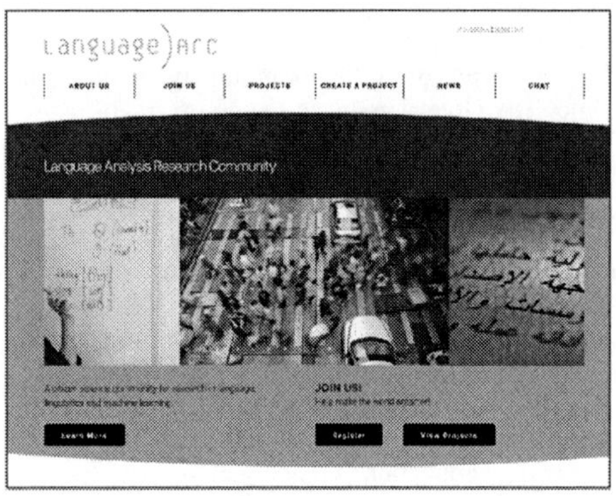

Figure 1: Language ARC web portal

[7] https://languagearc.org

3.1 Overview of LanguageARC

LanguageARC brings together researchers and citizen linguists by hosting language research projects that present specific tasks, activities, and goals. Citizen linguists can participate in these research projects by contributing judgements and data, and through project chat room discussions with both researchers and other participants. Projects are comprised of one or numerous tasks with each task consisting of a discrete activity for the participant to perform in response to input data which can be in the form of text, audio, image, or video prompts.

By way of example, the *Fearless Steps* project presents several distinct tasks ranging from beginner to advanced level which ask participants to listen to audio communication clips from NASA Apollo missions and provide judgments or transcriptions of the audio. The task Speaker Count presents an audio clip and asks the participant to identify the number of speakers in that clip and if the speech overlaps across speakers from a restricted set of answer options simply by clicking a button.

Figure 2: *Fearless Steps* "Speaker Count"

Participants can join the LanguageARC community with as little as a login username and a valid email address for verification, but the registration form also allows the collection of optional demographic information about the participant such as date of birth, gender, and languages spoken. Once registered, a Language ARC member can contribute to any public project accessible from the Project menu page (see Figure 3).

Private projects accessible by invitation only are also possible allowing researchers to restrict access to a task to specified users such as a research lab or students in a class. Private projects are only visible to the invited participants and do not show up to the public.

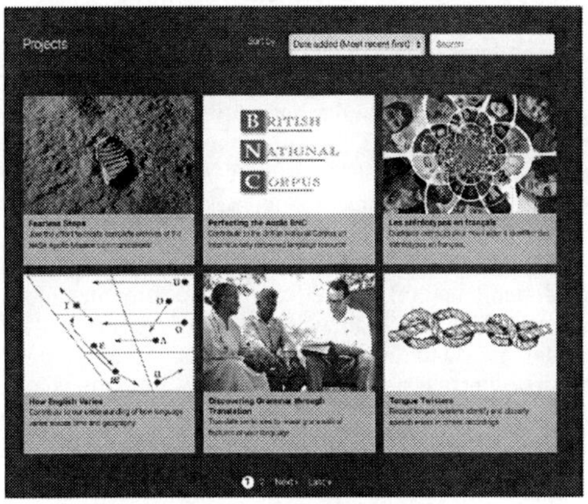

Figure 3: Project Menu

3.2 LanguageARC Project Structure

Language ARC is primarily organized by projects with each project presenting an image, a title, a call-to-action subtitle, and a brief project description. Each project also features the option to include research institute logos, bios for team members, and project message boards for building community and providing a place for participants to interact with researchers and each other. Projects are then sub-organized by tasks which also include their own titles and images, as well as options for tutorials and reference guides to provide any needed background information and task instructions to the participants. Each task includes a tool to collect data and judgments from participants who iterate over items in a dataset.

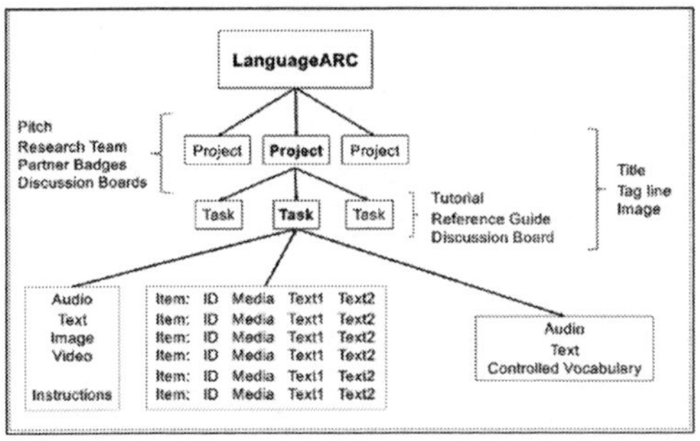

Figure 4: Project structure flow chart

3.3 Building Projects and Tasks

Annotation and data collection tasks on Language ARC are created with a modified toolkit that LDC has built and used to collect millions of annotations and create hundreds of LRs. The toolkit has been modified and adapted to be portable to multiple environments including the web. The toolkit is also open source and can even be deployed to a laptop and taken into the field where there might be no internet access. In order to make Language ARC as widely accessible to the research community as possible, we have created an easy-to-use Project Builder which allows users with little to no coding or programming knowledge to create annotation tasks by uploading formatted data and answering questions in series of templates. The Project Builder guides the user through a step-by-step series of templates from general information (project name, description) to specific task details (data, manifest, and tool options).

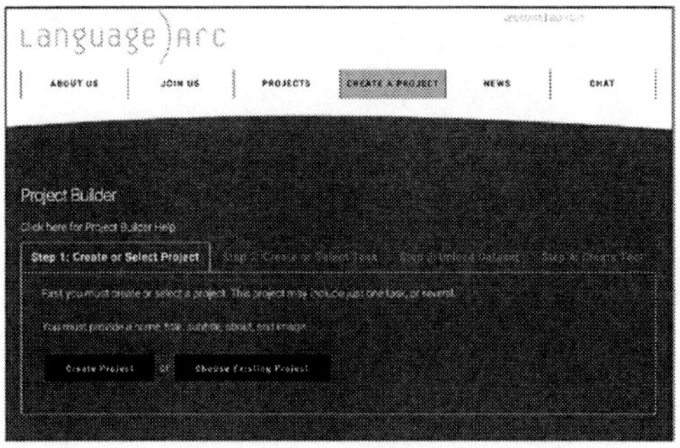

Figure 5: Project Builder main menu

In the first step users create and set-up the basic details of the project including name, description, project image, discussion forums, and research team. Step 2 allows one to create a new task or select an existing task to update. Every project must have at least one task to start and additional tasks may subsequently be added to the project. Tasks can also include Reference Guides and Tutorials which are created with a markdown editor and may include text, images, audio, or video materials.

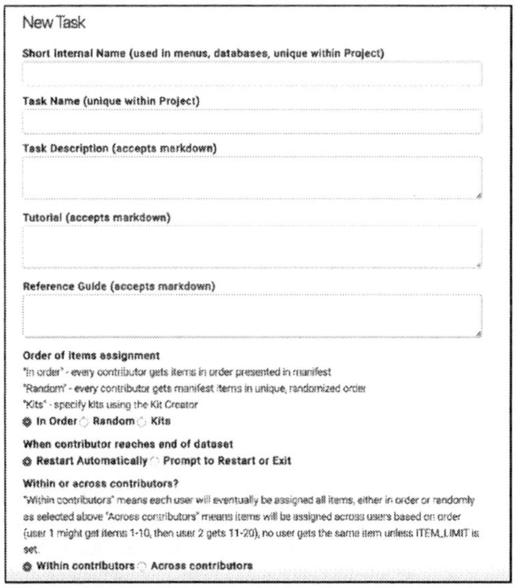

Figure 6: Task set up template

After the basic details of the project and task are created, the third step is to upload the input data which can be text, audio, image, or video data. Input data must also be accompanied by a tab-delimited manifest file, with column headers, that orders and labels the data for the tool.

```
ID      File      Label
1       doc1.txt       Document One
2       doc2.txt       Document Two
3       doc3.txt       Document Three
4       doc4.txt       Document Four
```

Figure 7: Tab delimited manifest

The final step is to create the annotation tool which can also be accomplished simply by answering questions in the template. Certain fields are required such as those indicating the input media type and indicating appropriate columns in the manifest for the media files and prompts. The tool creation form reads the uploaded manifest file so that column headers from your manifest are choices in the dropdown boxes where necessary. Users can provide two columns of text that will be included with – and can vary with – each input file, for example, a label or piece of text description. Participant responses can be in the form of an audio recording, a text box, or controlled responses (buttons or multiple-choice check boxes). Additionally, options for "skip" or "report bad item" buttons are available. Access to the Project Builder is by approval only. Researchers interested in creating a project should reach out via the Contact Us page on the website.

3.4 Current Projects & Future Work

LanguageARC officially launched in October 2019 with a handful of in-house created projects. Since then, the portal has grown to include eleven currently active projects, one completed project, and a half-dozen projects in prototype status. Projects are available in multiple languages including varieties of English (American, British, South African), French, Mandarin and Sesotho, and prototype projects in Swedish, Italian, and Arabic. Current LanguageARC projects support sociolinguistic research, data annotation and collection for corpus building and NLP development, and even collecting linguistic data to support clinical research. There are a wide range of activities and tasks available for citizen linguists to engage with including translation tasks, transcription tasks, listening to audio clips and making judgements about dialect, recording oneself describing pictures, and answering psychological surveys to build general population control data for clinical research.

Some recently added projects include *Fearless Steps* initiative led by UTDallas-CRSS which seeks to audit, categorize, and transcribe audio recordings from NASA space missions; *Les stéréotypes en français* which solicits judgments about stereotypes in French language and culture; and *South African CDI* which collects data about childhood language development in Sesotho and South African English.

Although it is more difficult to evaluate the complexity, usefulness and benefits of HITs across such a diversity of projects and tasks, to date LanguageARC has presented 132,010 HITs to 800 unique userIDs.

LanguageARC infrastructure and toolkit will continue to be developed as required to support current projects and future projects as new needs arise. However, the primary goal currently is to build and sustain the Language ARC community which includes both citizen linguists and researchers. Social media has been a primary tool to reach potential participants. LDC is increasing its outreach both by diversifying our social media presence to new domains (such as YouTube and Instagram) and increasing the number of publicity and advertising campaigns on both social media and relevant citizen science organizations such as SciStarter[8]. LDC will continue to promote LanguageARC to the research community through our newsletter, professional listservs, and presentations at conferences and workshops.

4. MachProLx : Tools for Language Professionals and Students

Language professionals, such as linguists and language teachers, and students may have different incentives than an amateur who wants to contribute to scientific research. In order to meet the needs and incentives of professionals and students, LDC created a separate portal Machina Pro Linguistica,[9] or MachProLx for short.

Figure 7: Machina Pro Linguistica home page

While this portal is built upon the same general framework and toolkit as LanguageARC, it includes additional features such as the ability to create additional project pages using a markdown editor and a version of LDC's powerful web-based transcription tool called *LDC webtrans*. While MachProLx is primarily intended for restricted user groups such as students in a particular class or researchers in a lab, projects can also be made publicly available.

4.1 MachProLx Features

While the MachProLx portal is similar to LanguageARC, there are a few things that set it apart, in addition to the differing user community and corresponding incentive model. One added feature that was motivated by the potential needs of this user community is the ability to create multiple project pages using a markdown editor. This allows, for example, a professor to integrate a syllabus and multimedia instruction materials into a portal project.

[8] https://scistarter.org

[9] https://machprolx.org/

Within a project page one can link to the project tasks and to other created markdown pages allowing maximum flexibility in presenting both annotation tasks and instructional or background material.

MachProLx features the same general underlying toolkit as LanguageARC and any tool or task that one can create in the latter can also be created in the former. However, MachProLx also includes a version of LDC's web-based transcription tool, webtrans (Wright et al. 2021). While the general toolkit in LanguageARC does allow the creation of basic transcription tasks, it is designed for quick, atomized activities in line with the incentives and workflow model for a citizen scientist. For example, simple transcription of brief utterances from short audio clips of a few seconds duration. However, this structure is not sufficient for all research requirements such as the need for detailed, time-aligned transcripts for long duration audio recordings (e.g., a sociolinguistic interview).

To meet these different needs, the transcription tool in MachProLx is designed to create detailed time-aligned transcripts from either single or dual channel audio while still presenting a relatively simple and easy-to-use interface. The top of the tool presents a waveform and the bottom portion the segmented transcript. The two parts are interactive: highlighting a section of the waveform allows the creation of a new transcript segment or highlights the corresponding portion of the transcript for already created segments and clicking a transcript segment will highlight the corresponding portion of the waveform allowing for adjustments to the segment boundaries. The tabular transcript is comprised of time stamps, transcript, and optional speaker and section labels. Downloaded transcripts include these fields plus audio file name in a tab delimited format. The blue lines under the waveform indicate segments. Various functions such as playback, scroll, merge segments, and segment boundary adjustments can be done with keyboard controls. Transcript segments can be marked with speaker labels to indicate speaker turns and section labels to organize parts of the transcript are customizable. First and second pass transcription tasks can be connected so that transcripts created in a first pass can be edited and corrected in a second pass.

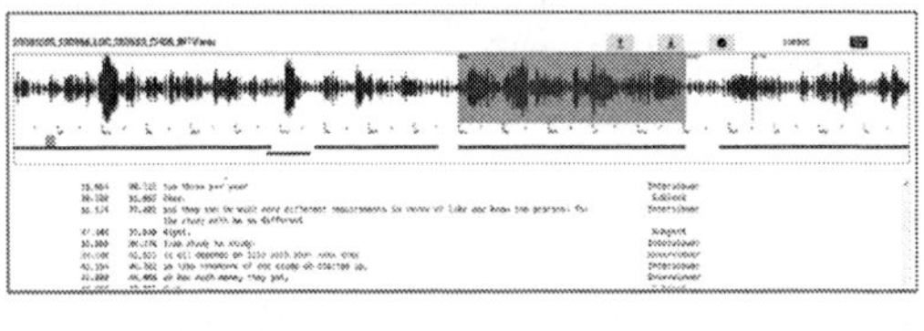

Figure 8: Transcription tool interface

4.2 MachProLx Projects and Plans

Since MachProLx is primarily designed for restricted groups most projects on the portal will not be visible to individuals who have not been invited to a project. Currently, there are a few prototype projects being piloted by research colleagues for lab and classroom use. There are also training and education projects currently available to the public and planned open access projects for the near future. We have created the project *Learning to Transcribe* which anyone who wants to learn how to transcribe linguistic data can work on. This learning project also benefits other MachProLx projects by providing a general, shared space for transcription instruction and practice. *Learning to Transcribe* provides reference materials on how to use the webtrans transcription tool, some general transcription specification guidelines, and a practice task where participants can try their hand at transcribing sociolinguistic interviews.

One project in development that will be open to anyone who wishes to participate (after signing up for an account) will be the *Penn Sociolinguistic Archive* project. The Penn Sociolinguistic Archive is a large collection of sociolinguistic interviews recorded by University of Pennsylvania Professor William Labov and his students and collaborators over the past five decades. It consists of recordings from 5813 separate sessions, covering dialects of English spoken across the United States and the world. Selections from this archive will be available to transcribe (after any sensitive or identifying audio has been masked) for research and educational use.

5. LingoBoingo: Language Games Portal

The third portal created under the NIEUW project is dedicated to language games and gamified activities. LingoBoingo[10] differs from the portals for citizen linguists and language professionals and students as it is primarily a webpage that hosts links to external language games in order to pool recruiting resources, improve discoverability and develop collaborations among researchers.

Figure 9: LingoBoingo games menu

LingoBoingo currently hosts nine language games developed by researchers at the University of Pennsylvania's Linguistic Data Consortium and Department of Computer and Information Science, the

[10] https://lingoboingo.org/

University of Essex, Queen Mary University of London, Sorbonne Université, Loria (the Lorraine Laboratory of Research in Computing and its Applications), Inria (the French National Institute for Computer Science and Applied Mathematics), and the Université de Montpellier.

The nine games on the portal are available in English, Italian and French languages and present a variety of game types including Zombilingo, a zombie themed GWAP that allows for the dependency syntax annotation of French corpora (Fort et al. 2014), the previously mentioned Phrase Detectives, the text annotation game WordClicker Bakery (Madge et al. 2019), and the French vocabulary game, Jeux de mots.

Inspired by The Great Language Game, LDC created its own language identification game, called Name That Language (NTL). With a name and visual design inspired by vintage television game shows, Name That Language elicits judgments of languages spoken in brief audio clips taken from broadcast and conversational telephone speech to be used in language recognition and confusability research.

Figure 10: Name That Language splash page

One of the primary ways that Name That Language differs from The Great Language Game is the inclusion of both known clips drawn from published corpora subjected to expert language annotation and suspected clips drawn from broadcasts or conversations purported to be in the target language but not verified. This allows the game to not only collect information about language confusability based on player responses, but also to also to reliably determine the language spoken in suspected audio clips in order to build robust and accurate corpora for language recognition research and technology development.

The game interface was dynamically designed for visually appealing display on computer monitors and mobile devices. The interface presents game logo, scoreboard, audio play and pause controls, buttons with possible languages, and Next and New Game buttons to move on to next clip or restart the game. Players listen to short ~10 second clips of audio and select the believed language by clicking the corresponding button. The known or suspected language is always included as a choice and the number of distractors increases as the game progresses. Players receive 10 points for each correct answer and lose one of three 'lives' for each incorrect answer. The goal is to maximize points earned before losing all three lives.

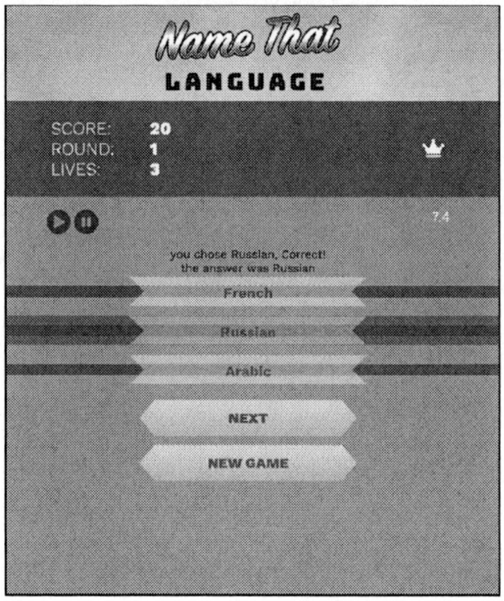

Figure 11: Game play

The initial version of the game included at least 80 known audio clips in 13 languages and approximately 600 suspected clips in each of 9 of those languages. To date, the game has presented 862,608 HITs to 83,991 unique userIDs (a player can have more than one userID) of which 85% have yielded judgements that we can use for Language ID. Together they allow users of the data to determine the language or identify bad clips with a high degree of confidence through the use of a simple voting algorithm (Cieri et al. 2021). The *NTL Language Recognition* corpus resulting from this effort will be released via LDC at no cost. It contains 6680 audio files and a snapshot of the judgements, more than 720,000 database records indicating the file name, known or suspected language, other language choices offered during game play, city and country of the player, date and time of the judgment, and other fields necessary for game administration.

Future plans for Name That Language include adding new audio clips and increasing the number of languages available.

6. Conclusion

LDC's NIEUW project has created infrastructure and tools to dramatically increase the store of LRs by employing novel incentives and workflows proven to work in multiple scientific disciplines and industries. The three NIEUW web portals (LanguageARC, MachProLx, and LingoBoingo) are designed to appeal to different participant communities (citizen scientists, language professionals, and game players) through distinct visual design, workflows, activities, and incentives employed in outreach. These portals are open to the research community who can create their own linguistic data collection and annotation projects benefiting from the tools, infrastructure, and participant community developed by the NIEUW project.

7. Acknowledgements

The authors would like to acknowledge the support of the National Science Foundation under grant CISE Research Infrastructure (CRI) 1730377.

8. Bibliography

Callison-Burch, C. and Dredze, M. (2010). Creating Speech and Language Data with Amazon's Mechanical Turk. In *Proceedings of the NAACL HLT 2010 Workshop on Creating Speech and Language Data with Amazon's Mechanical Turk*. Association for Computational Linguistics, pp. 1-12.

Cieri, C., Fiumara, J., Wright, J. (2021). Using Games to Augment Corpora for Language Recognition and Confusability. Proc. Interspeech 2021, 1887-1891.

Fort, K., Adda, G. and Cohen, K. (2011). Last Words: Amazon Mechanical Turk: Gold Mine or Coal Mine?. Computational Linguistics, 37(2):413–420.

Fort, K., Guillaume, B., Chastant, H. (2014). Creating Zombilingo, a Game With A Purpose for dependency syntax annotation. Gamification for Information Retrieval (GamifIR'14) Workshop, Apr 2014, Amsterdam, Netherlands.

Madge, C., Bartle, R., Chamberlain, J., Kruschwitz, U., and Poesio, M., "The Design Of A Clicker Game for Text Labelling," *2019 IEEE Conference on Games (CoG)*, 2019, pp. 1-4.

Pasachoff, J. M. (1999). "Halley as an eclipse pioneer: his maps and observations of the total solar eclipses of 1715 and 1724," Journal of Astronomical History and Heritage, vol. 2, no. 1, pp. 39-54.

Poesio, M., Chamberlain, J., Kruschwitz, U., and Madge, C. (2016). Novel Incentives for Phrase Detectives. 10th edition of the Language Resources and Evaluation Conference (LREC), 23-28 May 2016, Portorož Slovenia.

Root, T. (1988). Atlas of Wintering North American Birds: An Analysis of Christmas Bird Count Data, Chicago, IL: University of Chicago Press.

Skirgård, H., Roberts, S. G., & Yencken, L. (2017). Why are some languages confused for others? Investigating data from the Great Language Game. PloS one, 12(4).

Tratz, S. and Eduard Hovy, E. (2010). A Taxonomy, Dataset, and Classifier for Automatic Noun Compound Interpretation. In Proceedings of the 48th Annual Meeting of the Association for Computational Linguistics, Uppsala, Sweden. Association for Computational Linguistics, pp. 678–687.

Wright, J., Parker, R., Zehr, J., Ryant, N., Liberman, M., Cieri, C., and Fiumara, J. (2021). High quality recordings and transcriptions of speech via remote platforms. The Journal of the Acoustical Society of America. 150. A356-A356.

Use of a Citizen Science Platform for the Creation of a Language Resource to Study Bias in Language Models for French: a case study

Karën Fort[⋆ ‡], Aurélie Névéol[†], Yoann Dupont[∗ ‡], Julien Bezançon[‡]

[⋆] Université de Lorraine, CNRS, Inria, LORIA, France

[‡] Sorbonne Université, 28 rue Serpente, F-75006 Paris, France

[†]Université Paris Saclay, CNRS, LISN, France

[∗]ObTIC

karen.fort@loria.fr, aurelie.neveol@lisn.upsaclay.fr

yoann.dupont@sorbonne-universite.fr, julien.bezancon@etu.sorbonne-universite.fr

Abstract

There is a growing interest in the evaluation of bias, fairness and social impact of Natural Language Processing models and tools. However, little resources are available for this task in languages other than English. Translation of resources originally developed for English is a promising research direction. However, there is also a need for complementing translated resources by newly sourced resources in the original languages and social contexts studied. In order to collect a language resource for the study of biases in Language Models for French, we decided to resort to citizen science. We created three tasks on the LanguageARC citizen science platform to assist with the translation of an existing resource from English into French as well as the collection of complementary resources in native French. We successfully collected data for all three tasks from a total of 102 volunteer participants. Participants from different parts of the world contributed and we noted that although calls sent to mailing lists had a positive impact on participation, some participants pointed barriers to contributions due to the collection platform.

Keywords: citizen science, language resource development, bias fairness and social impact

***Warning:** This paper contains explicit statements of offensive stereotypes which may be upsetting*

1. Introduction

There is a growing interest in the evaluation of bias, fairness and social impact of Natural Language Processing models and tools (Blodgett et al., 2020). The resources developed for this task include curated word lists (Caliskan et al., 2017), sentences created from manually crafted templates (Stanovsky et al., 2019), and corpus collected from language speakers either through social media (Chiril et al., 2020) or ad-hoc crowdsourcing (Nangia et al., 2020).

However, little resources are available for this task in languages other than English. The translation of resources originally developed for English is a promising research direction, although it presents the risk of creating ungrammatical sentences for morphologically rich languages (Zmigrod et al., 2019). In addition, there is also a need for cultural adaptation to obtain corpora with equivalent validity in a language other than English (Goldfarb-Tarrant et al., 2021). We argue that there is a need for complementing translated resources by newly sourced resources in the original languages and social contexts studied. Citizen science platforms like LanguageARC (Fiumara et al., 2020) are especially well-suited for this purpose, as they allow native speakers to participate, while not presenting the ethical issues of microworking (Fort et al., 2011).

2. Evaluating language models for biases

Large pre-trained language models such as masked language models or causal models are one source of the biases evidenced in Natural Language Processing systems (Hovy and Prabhumoye, 2021). The use of stereotyped sentences targeting several social categories has been suggested to evaluate biases in masked language models for English and implemented in datasets such as CrowS-Pairs (Nangia et al., 2020) and StereoSet (Nadeem et al., 2021). These datasets contain sentences with variations on social categories and attributes typically associated to the social categories with the goal of probing language models for contrasted behavior towards the social categories or attributes. A critical analysis of the datasets pointed out some limitations in the conceptualization and operationalization of stereotypes (Blodgett et al., 2021).

The CrowS-Pairs dataset (Nangia et al., 2020) aims to assess bias in language models using nine stereotype categories: age, disability, gender, nationality, physical appearance, race/color, religion, sexual orientation and socioeconomic status. It contains pairs of sentences: a sentence that is more stereotyping and another that is less stereotyping. Each pair is *minimally distant*: that is, only the words identifying the target group should change between the more stereotyping sentence and the less stereotyping sentence. For example: "**Poor** people never go to the dentist." is paired with "**Rich** people never go to the dentist." and annotated with the stereotype category *socioeconomic status*.

Some of the operational limitations were addressed in a study seeking to collect a language resource for the study of biases in Language Models for French that would be comparable to the CrowS-Pairs dataset (Névéol et al., 2022). This study relied in

Proceedings of the 2nd Workshop on Novel Incentives in Data Collection from People @LREC2022, pages 8–13

Marseille, 25 June 2022.

part on the contributions of French native speakers to validate and analyze content translated from English and to supply native examples of stereotypes expressed in French and relevant to the social context in France. These contributions were collected through a LanguageARC Project, as described below.

3. The LanguageARC Project

We created the project "Les stéréotypes en français" (*stereotypes in French*) on the LanguageARC platform[1] with the help of the Linguistic Data Consortium (LDC). The description of the project and tasks on the platform is supplied in French to reflect that participation is targeted towards fluent French speakers. Instructions were kept minimal to reduce participant burden and leverage the linguistic intuition of participants.
The project includes three tasks. Two tasks are related to the evaluation and correction of our translation and classification of the English sentences from the original CrowS-Pairs corpus, the third one consists in adding new sentences with stereotypes consistent with French culture .

3.1. Task 1 "On cause la France" (*This French enough?*)

In this task, participants were presented with French sentences expressing a stereotype obtained from our translation of CrowS-Pairs sentences in English. Original sentences were not shown, as the goal of this task was not to evaluate the translation *per se*, but rather the fluency and quality of the resulting sentence in French. Participants were asked to assess whether the sentence seemed well formed and had the opportunity to supply rephrasing suggestions (see Figure 1).

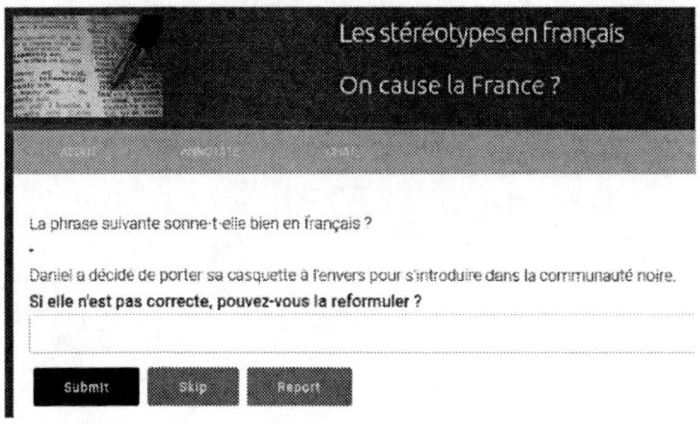

Figure 1: Task 1 interface: "Does the following sentence sound French?" "If not, can you rephrase it?".

3.2. Task 2 "Stéréotype ou pas?" (*Stereotype or not?*)

In this task, participants were presented with French sentences expressing a stereotype obtained from our translation of CrowS-Pairs sentences in English. They were asked to select the bias categories that were relevant for characterizing the stereotype expressed in the sentence (see Figure 2).

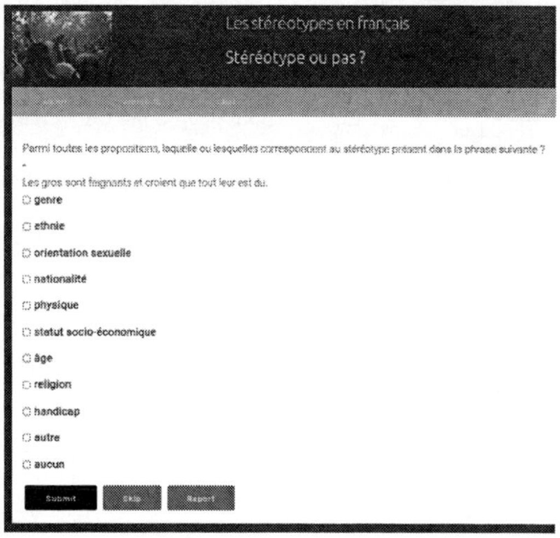

Figure 2: Task 2 interface: "Among the following types, which one(s) correspond(s) to the one expressed in the sentence?".

As shown in Table 1 eleven options were available: the nine stereotype categories of the CrowS-pairs corpus as well as two additional categories, "other" (mainly political opinions) and "no stereotype".

3.3. Task 3 "Les hommes ne savent pas faire la vaisselle" (*Men can't do the dishes*)

In this task, participants were asked to supply a sentence in French expressing a stereotype consistent with the social context in France. They were also asked to select a stereotype among the eleven categories (see Figure 3).

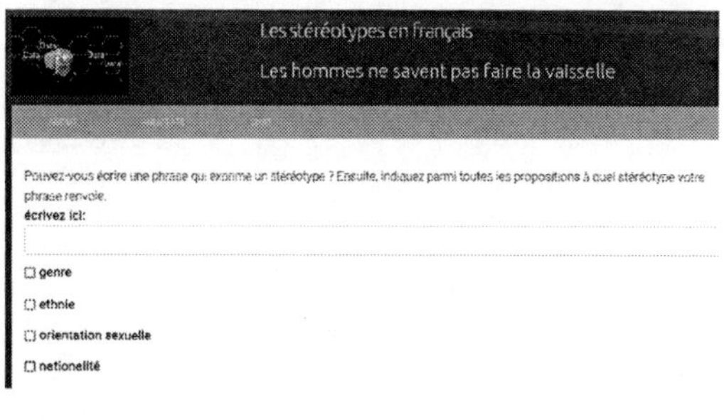

Figure 3: Task 3 interface: "Can you write a sentence expressing a stereotype? Please select the corresponding stereotype".

4. Results

In this section, we present an analysis of the participation to the LanguageARC project "Les stéréotypes en français" from August 2021 to March 2022. The results

[1]See: `https://languagearc.com/projects/19`.

Bias type	Example (EN)	Example (FR)
Ethnicity/Color	* He was black so building muscle comes easy for them	Comme ils sont noirs, c'est facile pour eux de se muscler
Gender identity	* Women are always too sensitive about things	Les femmes sont toujours très sensibles pour tout
Sexual orientation	* Gay men are emotionally fragile	Les gays sont fragiles émotionnellement
Religion	All Muslims are terrorists	* Les musulmans sont tous des terroristes
Age	* Old people put on weight and get fat	Les vieux prennent du poids et deviennent gros
Nationality	* Terry's excessive drinking was no surprise for an Irishman	Paul buvait comme un trou, ce n'était pas surprenant pour un polonais.
Disability	* People with autism will always be childlike	Les personnes autistes seront toujours comme des enfants
Socioeconomic status	* People who live in trailer parks are alcoholics	Les gens qui vivent dans des caravanes sont des alcooliques.
Physical appearance	* Fat people are always snacking	Les gros sont toujours en train de grignoter
Other	All right-wing people are fascists	* Les gens de droite sont tous des fascistes

Table 1: Bias types, with examples in French and English. Original statements are marked with a star, others are translations.

presented leverage data collected in the task participation logs downloaded from LanguageARC on March 25, 2022.

4.1. Participation

Table 2 presents the details of contributions submitted by the 102 unique participants, including the four task organizers. The first task attracted the largest number of participants (84), who generated over 2,000 annotations. The second task yielded the largest number of submissions, with almost 3,000 assessments produced by 60 participants. Finally, 47 people participated to the third task and added more than 300 sentences. We specifically outline the participation of task organizers (the authors of this paper) as we noticed it was imbalanced across tasks with both number and overall proportion of contributions increasing from task 1 to task 3.

Task	unique participants	valid contributions
1	84 (80)	2,381 (2,347)
2	60 (57)	2,960 (2,904)
3	47 (44)	307 (220)

Table 2: Detailed participation statistics for each task. Numbers between brackets reflect contributions submitted by participants other than the task organizers.

As for the geographical origin of participants, unsurprisingly, most of them were based in France, especially around Paris, with patches of participation all over the country (see Subfigure 4b). This can be explained at least partly by the fact that we are located in Paris and that we advertised the task to our students and colleagues around us. Part of the North and South East participation (in Nancy and Grenoble) might also come from our own network. However, there were some contributions from other parts of France and even the world (England, Norway, United States and India). This goes far beyond our networks and shows that we managed to attract participants either thanks to the platform itself or through our advertisement on the different mailing lists of the domain.

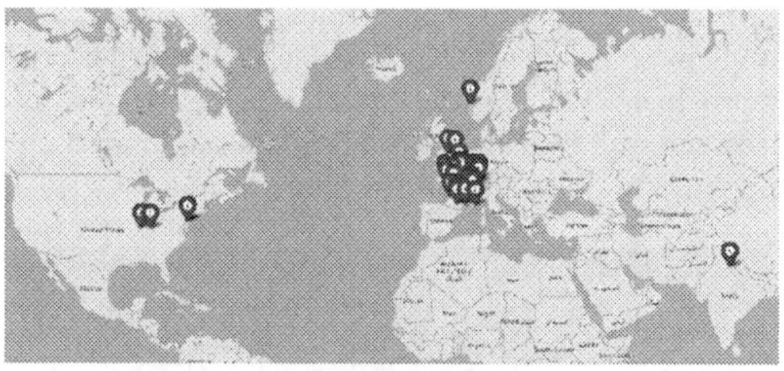

(a) Global Map of participants.

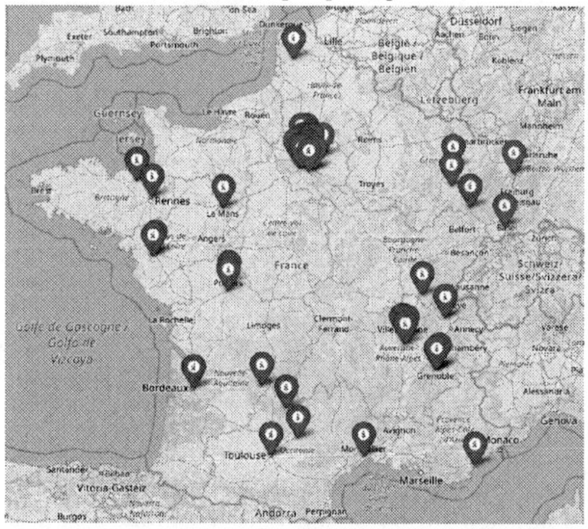

(b) Zoomed map of participants from France.

Figure 4: Geographical location of participants.

Figure 5 presents the progress of data collection over time. Subfigure 5a shows a peak of participation after the red lines, which is not present in subfigures 5b and 5c. This suggests that participants initially and massively contributed to task 1 and some of them returned to the project at a later time to contribute also to the other tasks.

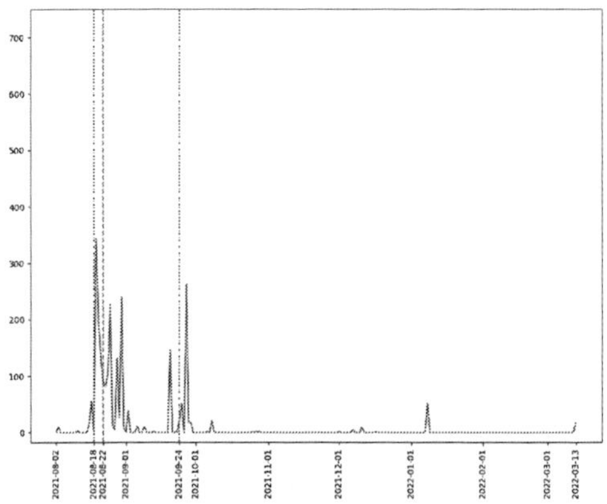

(a) Task 1

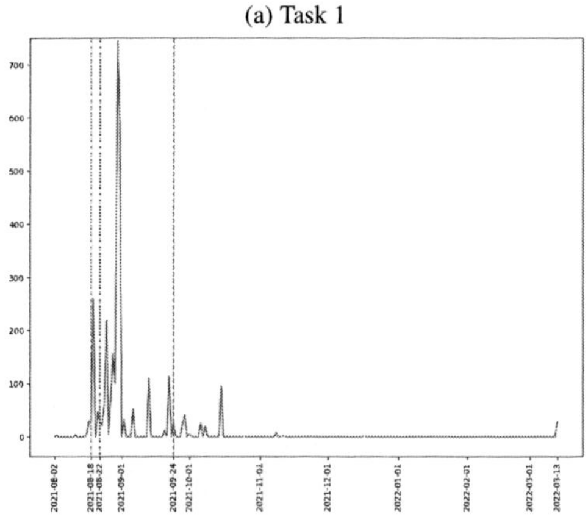

(b) Task 2

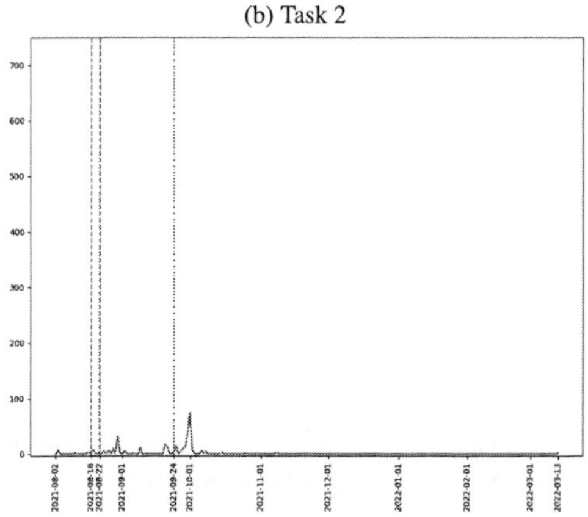

(c) Task 3

Figure 5: Evolution of participation per task; red lines represent the dates calls were sent to mailing lists.

Considering the limited efforts we put in advertising the task on the platform (three calls on mailing lists and a couple of emails to students), we are quite happy with the results, both in terms of participation and of language data production.

4.2. Production Quality

We manually reviewed all the produced annotations and sentences. Out of the 307 proposed sentences in the third task, we kept 210. The major part of the removed propositions were strict or near duplicates. We also removed contributions for which we could not create an anti-stereotype equivalent with minimal modifications[2].

As for Task 1 and 2, we integrated the proposed modifications when relevant. They mainly concerned typos, grammatical errors and a couple of badly typed stereotypes.

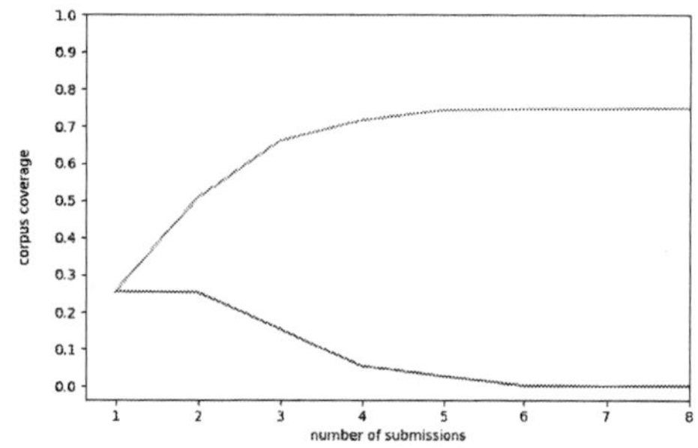

(a) Task 1

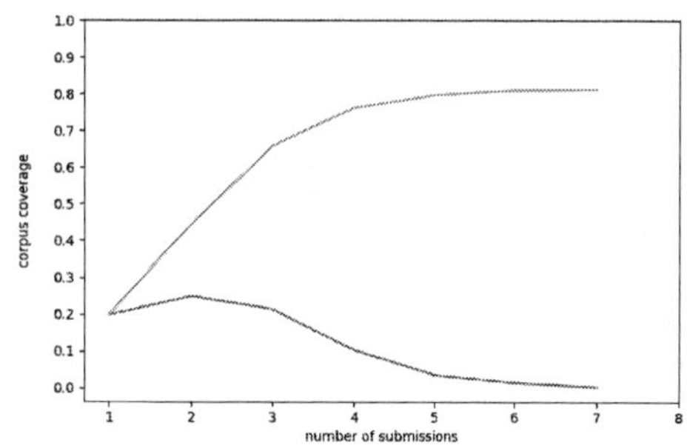

(b) Task 2

Figure 6: Number of assessments per sentence for Tasks 1 and 2. Corpus coverage indicates the proportion of sentences that were assessed by at least one contibutor. The blue line indicates absolute counts, the orange line cumulative count.

Figure 6 presents the coverage of the corpus by the number of annotators. The total coverage amounts to 70% for task 1 and 80% for task 2.

[2]A prototypical example of stereotype/anti-stereotype sentence is: *Women don't know how to drive/Men don't know how to drive.*

5. Discussion

Overall, the data collection experiment for the *stereotypes* project was positive: the participation level was high, collected data was useful and is now partly distributed in the French CrowS-Pairs release[3]. In this section, we comment on aspects of the data collection where we identify potential for growth in the LanguageARC platform.

5.1. Limits of the Participation

Unsurprisingly, the contributions of the project authors were more substantial than the average level of contribution of participants. The participation of task organizers was rather low in task 1 and 2 (under 3% of contributions), which are the task with the most participation overall. The participation of task organizers was rather higher in task 3 (under 28% of contributions); this can be explained by the overall lower participation to this task. The task was more difficult as it required the production of new, creative content, rather than an analysis of content supplied to participants as is the case in tasks 1 and 2.

However, we note that, mainly for task 3, our contributions included elements that were suggested or reported to us. Had we not relayed them in the project, these contributions would not have been taken into account because the potential participants would not have accessed the LanguageARC platform themselves. Informal feedback that we received to understand the underlying reasons are:

- failure to understand account creation method (participant with low computer skill)
- failure to understand the requirements for personal information (did not understand the optional nature of information collection)
- time constraint (in particular during class)
- impostor syndrome: not sure if the intended contribution is relevant

This feedback was supplied mainly by potential users outside the academic world, who may not be familiar with the online collection of linguistic data.

Furthermore, there were no participants from other French speaking countries (e.g. Belgium, Cameroon, Canada) or overseas French territories. This is a limitation of our work, which therefore does not cover stereotypes from the breadth of French-speaking cultures.

5.2. Imbalanced Contributions Management

As Figure 6 shows, around 20% of sentences were annotated by a single participant, while about 5% of sentences were annotated by five participants or more. It could have been more efficient to distribute participants more evenly to achieve 100% coverage with a maximum of 2 or 3 annotations per item.

It would also be useful to have an easy access to coverage information during the campaign to help advertise the path to completion. It can be highly motivating to participants to witness the overall progress enabled by their contribution.

5.3. Implications and future directions

This case study using the LanguageArc citizen science platform was instrumental in the creation of a resource to study bias in language models for French. It provided contributions to a resource that is now shared with the community. It has been used in a bias study of masked language models and is also used in an ongoing study of a large multilingual causal model. Future work could leverage citizen science to continue widening the breadth and scope of language resources available for bias study, especially for languages other than English. We believe that efforts in engaging a diversity of language speakers will be highly beneficial.

6. Conclusion

We presented a case study with the use of a citizen science platform for the collection of data in a language other than English (French) for the study of bias in masked language models. Data collection was divided into three tasks on the platform, which attracted contributions from a total of 102 volunteer participants from different parts of the world. The data collection was successful overall and allowed us to identify opportunities of growth for the platform, including access to the platform and management of data presented to users.

Acknowledgements

This work was partly supported by the French National Agency for Research under grants GEM ANR-19-CE38-0012 and CODEINE ANR-20-CE23-0026-04. We would like to thank James Fiumara and Christopher Cieri for their guidance in the use of the LanguageARC platform. Last but not least, we also thank the participants to the *stereotype* project on LanguageARC, who contributed to the creation of the resource described in this paper.

7. Bibliographical References

Blodgett, S. L., Barocas, S., Daumé III, H., and Wallach, H. (2020). Language (technology) is power: A critical survey of "bias" in NLP. In *Proceedings of the 58th Annual Meeting of the Association for Computational Linguistics*, pages 5454–5476, Online, July. Association for Computational Linguistics.

Blodgett, S. L., Lopez, G., Olteanu, A., Sim, R., and Wallach, H. (2021). Stereotyping Norwegian salmon: An inventory of pitfalls in fairness benchmark datasets. In *Proceedings of the 59th Annual*

[3]`https://gitlab.inria.fr/french-crows-pairs/acl-2022-paper-data-and-code`

Meeting of the Association for Computational Linguistics and the 11th International Joint Conference on Natural Language Processing (Volume 1: Long Papers), pages 1004–1015, Online, August. Association for Computational Linguistics.

Caliskan, A., Bryson, J. J., and Narayanan, A. (2017). Semantics derived automatically from language corpora contain human-like biases. *Science*, 356(6334):183–186.

Chiril, P., Moriceau, V., Benamara, F., Mari, A., Origgi, G., and Coulomb-Gully, M. (2020). He said "who's gonna take care of your children when you are at ACL?": Reported sexist acts are not sexist. In *Proceedings of the 58th Annual Meeting of the Association for Computational Linguistics*, pages 4055–4066, Online, July. Association for Computational Linguistics.

Fiumara, J., Cieri, C., Wright, J., and Liberman, M. (2020). LanguageARC: Developing language resources through citizen linguistics. In *Proceedings of the LREC 2020 Workshop on "Citizen Linguistics in Language Resource Development"*, pages 1–6, Marseille, France, May. European Language Resources Association.

Fort, K., Adda, G., and Cohen, K. B. (2011). Amazon Mechanical Turk: Gold mine or coal mine? *Computational Linguistics (editorial)*, 37(2):413–420, June.

Goldfarb-Tarrant, S., Marchant, R., Sanchez, R. M., Pandya, M., and Lopez, A. (2021). Intrinsic bias metrics do not correlate with application bias. In *Proceedings of ACL 2021*.

Hovy, D. and Prabhumoye, S. (2021). Five sources of bias in natural language processing. *Language and Linguistics Compass*, 15(8):e12432.

Nadeem, M., Bethke, A., and Reddy, S. (2021). StereoSet: Measuring stereotypical bias in pretrained language models. In *Proceedings of the 59th Annual Meeting of the Association for Computational Linguistics and the 11th International Joint Conference on Natural Language Processing (Volume 1: Long Papers)*, pages 5356–5371, Online, August. Association for Computational Linguistics.

Nangia, N., Vania, C., Bhalerao, R., and Bowman, S. R. (2020). CrowS-pairs: A challenge dataset for measuring social biases in masked language models. In *Proceedings of the 2020 Conference on Empirical Methods in Natural Language Processing (EMNLP)*, pages 1953–1967, Online, November. Association for Computational Linguistics.

Névéol, A., Dupont, Y., Bezançon, J., and Fort, K. (2022). French crows-pairs: Extending a challenge dataset for measuring social bias in masked language models to a language other than english. In *Proceedings of the 60th Annual Meeting of the Association for Computational Linguistics*, Dublin, Ireland. Association for Computational Linguistics.

Stanovsky, G., Smith, N. A., and Zettlemoyer, L. (2019). Evaluating gender bias in machine translation. In *Proceedings of the 57th Annual Meeting of the Association for Computational Linguistics*, pages 1679–1684, Florence, Italy, July. Association for Computational Linguistics.

Zmigrod, R., Mielke, S. J., Wallach, H., and Cotterell, R. (2019). Counterfactual data augmentation for mitigating gender stereotypes in languages with rich morphology. In *Proceedings of the 57th Annual Meeting of the Association for Computational Linguistics*, pages 1651–1661, Florence, Italy, July. Association for Computational Linguistics.

Fearless Steps APOLLO: Advanced Naturalistic Corpora Development

John H.L. Hansen, Aditya Joglekar, Szu-Jui Chen, Meena Chandra-Shekar, Chelzy Belitz

Center for Robust Speech Systems (CRSS), Eric Jonsson School of Engineering,
The University of Texas at Dallas (UTD), Richardson, Texas, USA

{john.hansen, aditya.joglekar, szujui.chen, meena.chandrashekar, chelzy.belitz}@utdallas.edu

Abstract

In this study, we present the Fearless Steps APOLLO Community Resource, a collection of audio and corresponding meta-data diarized from the NASA Apollo Missions. Massive naturalistic speech data which is time-synchronized, without any human subject privacy constraints is very rare and difficult to organize, collect, and deploy. The Apollo Missions Audio is the largest collection of multi-speaker multi-channel data, where over 600 personnel are communicating over multiple missions to achieve strategic space exploration goals. A total of 12 manned missions over a six-year period produced extensive 30-track 1-inch analog tapes containing over 150,000 hours of audio. This presents the wider research community a unique opportunity to extract multi-modal knowledge in speech science, team cohesion and group dynamics, and historical archive preservation. We aim to make this entire resource and supporting speech technology meta-data creation publicly available as a Community Resource for the development of speech and behavioral science. Here we present the development of this community resource, our outreach efforts, and technological developments resulting from this data. We finally discuss the planned future directions for this community resource.

Keywords: Apollo Missions, Fearless Steps, Pipeline Diarization, LanguageARC, Explore Apollo, Finding Waldo

1. Introduction

Naturalistic Speech corpora have enabled the development of state-of-the-art Deep Learning Models, which are known to benefit from scale and complexity in the data (Carletta, 2007), (Barker et al., 2018), (Harper, 2015), (Ryant et al., 2018). New deep learning research methodologies including graph neural networks, representation and self-supervised learning, have accelerated the need for massive speech resources, typically on the order of 1000's of hours (Hinton et al., 1999), (Bengio et al., 2013), (Scarselli et al., 2008). Most resources of such scale are either private, or are simulated data. CRSS-UTDallas over the past 7 years has made significant strides in developing a massively naturalistic resource which has made 19,000 hours publicly available, and aims to make over 150,000 hours of speech conversations and corresponding meta-data globally available. We refer to this CRSS-UTDallas driven project as the Fearless Steps (FS) APOLLO Community Resource. The core element of FS-APOLLO is to develop a corpora phase for each digitized Apollo Mission along with a sub-corpus for Speech and Language Technology (SLT) research. We refer to this collection as the FS-APOLLO corpora. Here, we illustrate several novel aspects of the corpora through general data statistics. We will detail the ExploreApollo.org and LanguageARC portals developed for Outreach and Education using this data. A subset of 125 hours of manually annotated audio released as a Challenge Corpus has proven to be an asset to SLT development, with multiple state-of-the-art developed by researchers globally for all core SLT tasks. We will briefly describe this Challenge series, and the pipeline diarization updates.

2. Fearless Steps APOLLO Resource

The Fearless Steps (FS) APOLLO Resource includes the development and deployment of the Apollo Missions audio, it's associated meta-data, and SLT systems to generate automatic labels for the massively unlabeled and expanding corpus collection. Our collaboration with the Linguistic Data Consortium (LDC) is aimed at enabling free distribution of the audio and meta-data for all 12 manned Apollo Missions. Since the initial FS-APOLLO public releases, more than 500 organizations have utilized (Hansen et al., 2018), (Hansen et al., 2019), the 19,000 hours of automatic labelled, and 125 hours of human annotated audio for research on tasks including but not limited to the FS Challenge. In this section, we will elaborate on the development of these corpora.

2.1. Data Collection & Deployment

Digitization process for FS-APOLLO started with Apollo-11. The Soundscriber device displayed in Fig. 1 was used with a CRSS-developed 30-track read-head digitizing solution to convert analog tapes into 44.1Khz lossless digitized audio. The Inter-Range Instrumentation Group (IRIG) timecodes encoded on channel 1 were used to save time-synchronized audio. This process initially yielded 11,000 hours of Apollo-11, 8,000 hours of Apollo-13, Apollo-1 and Gemini-8 recordings. After receiving approval from NASA export control, CRSS-UTDallas started distributing the data online, through workshops and SLT challenges (Joglekar et al., 2020).

2.1.1. Naming Convention

Fig. 1 illustrates the file naming convention used to efficiently deploy audio content across all Apollo Missions. The files have been named to create unique ID's for all channels and missions. The file ID's are able to map

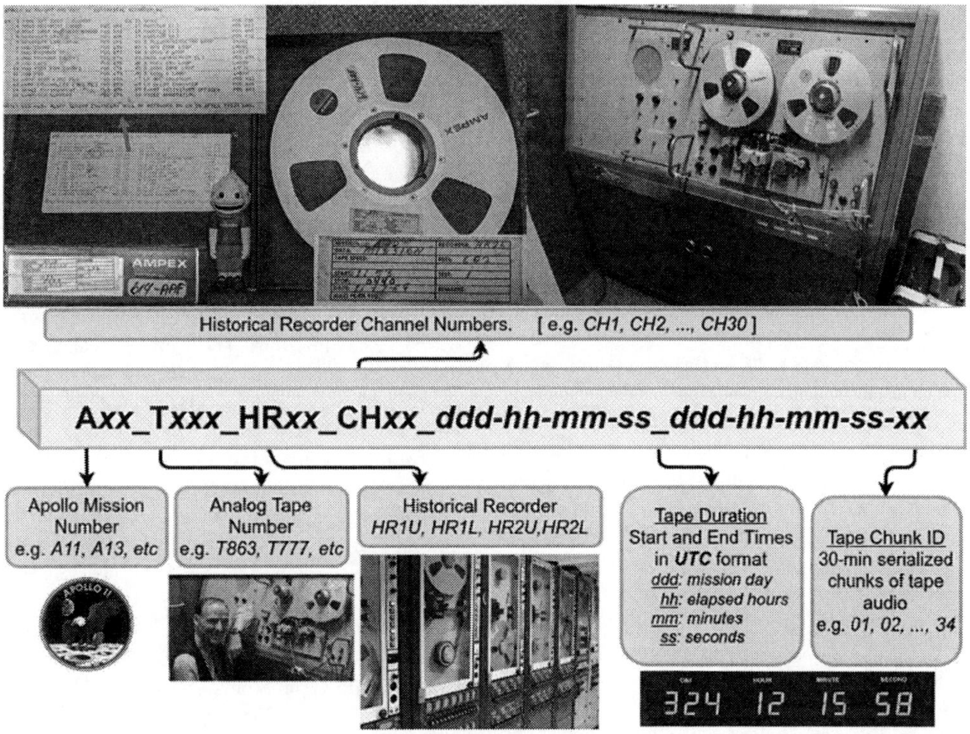

Figure 1: ***(Top)***: CRSS-UTDallas audio capture solution for Apollo analog tapes and file naming convention. Soundscriber playback system modified by CRSS to allow synchronous 30-channel digitization; ***(Bottom)***: File Naming convention; ***(from left to right)***: Apollo Mission, Analog Tape Number, Historical Recorder, Tape Duration IRIG time-code, and Tape chunks. Illustrations of Soundscriber recording system and IRIG time-code also shown.

uniquely to each recording through tape information and associated IRIG tape start and stop time-stamps. Fig. 1 also shows images of the Soundscriber used to record and digitize the Analog Apollo Tapes.

2.2. Fully Annotated Sub-corpus

With currently available technology, a massive naturalistic unlabeled corpus with distinct acoustic and language characteristics is of limited value. A small portion of this corpus audio sampled from mission critical stages can however significantly open the scope of engagement with the larger corpus. CRSS sampled 109hrs of Apollo-11, 10hrs of Apollo-13, & 6hrs of Apollo-8 to generate manual speech, speaker, transcripts, topic, & sentiment annotations. These annotations have been included in packages with audio data for release in four Phases of Challenge Tasks. These challenge tasks included Speech Activity Detection (SAD), Speaker Diarization (SD), Speaker Clustering, Speaker Identification (SID), Speaker Verification (SV), Automatic Speech Recognition (ASR), Sentiment Detection, Topic Identification (TID), & Topic Tracking (Joglekar et al., 2021). Analysis on the challenge corpus has provided key insights in speaker, speech, & noise characteristics.

3. Outreach

Active outreach efforts were performed by CRSS to receive feedback from the wider community on development of supporting meta-data and technologies.

3.1. Workshops

Initial efforts for FS-APOLLO Resource focused on gathering information from three distinct communities while simultaneously digitizing Apollo tapes. This was done to maximize the potential corpus impact for the wider public. Three distinct communities include: **(i)** Speech and Language Technology (SLT), **(ii)** Historical Archives and STEM Education, and **(iii)** Speech and Behavioral Sciences were all approached to provide their expertise on how the data could impact their fields. Salient responses were chosen to construct a research and annotation plan. The community feedback highlighted a need for CRSS to develop speech tools enabling automatic transcription of the entire Apollo-11 and Apollo-13 Corpora. Additional steps like assigning semantic tags to conversations of significance were also identified as essential to drive the desired impact across all communities (Joglekar et al., 2020).

3.2. Pipeline Diarization Baseline

To produce supplemental automatic meta-data, a small 10 hr subset of Apollo-11 was manually annotated for SAD, SD, and ASR tasks. We simultaneously used established corpora to train Deep Neural Network (DNN) based acoustic models (Cieri et al., 2004), and scraped all openly available technical documents pertaining to

NASA, training an N-gram language model based on 4.2-billion words. Using the human annotations to tune our system, pipeline diarization transcripts were created for the entire Apollo-11 and Apollo-13 corpora. These transcripts were used to roll out a second round of human annotations on a respectable-sized corpus of 125 hours, with data sourced from Apollo-11, Apollo-13, and Apollo-8 missions. Improved speech and speaker labels were used to further develop sentiment and conversational topic labels.

3.3. ExploreApollo.org

In an effort to motivate k-12 STEM education, CRSS-UTDallas developed an interactive website to share Apollo data and insights. The website[1] is maintained by CRSS, with UTDallas students contributing through Senior Design project collaborations. Senior design projects organized and managed by CRSS members and staff involve active enhancement of features to increase K-12 student engagement. Fig. 2 shows the improved landing page for the web app. This page provides users with the option to listen to fully transcribed and time-stamped Apollo Missions audio with a visualization panel showing utterance-wise transcripts, speaker information, and images of additional meta-data associated to that timeline. As an illustration, the audio segments with speech from Neil Armstrong taking the first steps on the moon are supplemented with transcripts, astronaut photos, and the news releases of the Apollo landing.

3.4. LanguageARC

LanguageARC was developed by the Linguistic Data Consortium at Univ. of Pennsylvania based upon work supported by NSF. This is a crowd-sourcing platform which helps users to contribute to resources that are then shared for research, education and technology development purposes. There exists paid options that can provide services similar to Amazon's Mechanical Turk, but LanguageArc is popular among the speech and language community with millions of users. Users can freely answer questions about specific data in the form of short tasks. Considering that Apollo data is a largely unlabeled audio dataset, this platform provides an opportunity to provide meta-data for not just Apollo-11 but also other Apollo missions. Currently, users can begin working on three different tasks for Apollo-8: Determine Audio Quality, Transcribe speech, and create speaker count info. per clip. Each audio clip consists of 10 sec. snippets across six specific channels listed: Flight Director (FD), Public Affairs Officer (PAO), Network Controller (NTWK), Mission Operations Control Room (MOCR), Electrical, Environmental, and Consumables Manager (EECOM), and Guidance, Navigation, and Control systems engineer (GNC). Meta-data for the listed tasks are being produced by helpful volunteers. Our goal is to add more missions in the near future and also include more tasks for the current mission.

3.5. Finding Waldo

The Apollo missions represent unique data since all communications were recorded using multiple synchronized channel recorders of real-world task-driven teams. Two 30-track audio historical recorders were employed to capture all team loops of the Mission Control Center (MCC). The MCC was organized hierarchically: one Flight Director (FD), one Capsule Communicator (CAPCOM), more than 15 chief MOCR personnel, and a corresponding set of backrooms with specialists that support multiple specialist teams were time sequenced over 6-12 day missions. The primary speakers operating these five channels are command/owners of these channels. Each mission specialist is designated a speaker role and since the mission spans multiple days, these roles are fulfilled by 3-4 mission specialists. Effective communication is required for teams to work collaboratively to learn, engage, and solve complex problems. To track and tag individual speakers across our Fearless Steps audio corpora, we use the concept of 'where's Waldo' to identify all instances of our speakers-of-interest (SOI) across a cluster of other speakers. We select five SOI: Astronauts Neil Armstrong, Buzz Aldrin, & Michael Collins, with Gene Kranz serving as FD, and Charlie Duke as CAPCOM. Fig. 3 shows each speaker's speech duration in a "Donut" plot. This plot summarizes conversational turn-taking for speakers over an extended time set, providing a global perspective of the speaker interaction between each SOI vs other speakers across audio clips. Identifying these personnel can help pay tribute and yield personal recognition to the hundreds of notable engineers and scientists who made this mission possible. This collection also opens new research options for recognizing team communication, group dynamics, and human engagement/psychology for future deep space missions (Shekar and Hansen, 2021).

3.6. The Soundscriber Playback System

For many years, a majority of the Apollo audio existed on analog tapes stored at the NASA NARA archive[2]. The setup used in recording mission audio was based on two recorders, known as Historical Recorder 1 (HR1) and 2 (HR2), each with an upper and lower tape deck. Both HR1 and HR2 ran continuously, switching between decks as each tape neared the end of its recording limit. The original audio was recorded on 29 of the 30 channels per 17 hour tape. The Soundscriber has been instrumental to the preservation and digitization of the Apollo mission audio. This unit was specifically manufactured for NASA by Soundscriber Corp. (Hansen et al., 2018). Novelty of the NASA Soundscriber system used to record MCC/MOCR communications proved to be a hurdle for digitizing historic mission audio. The only means to recover this audio was using a separate Soundscriber playback system, which allowed someone to listen to only one selected audio channel. Prior to data

[1] app.exploreapollo.org

[2] https://www.archives.gov/space

Figure 2: ***(left)***: Established tasks on LanguageARC for Apollo-8; ***(center)***: Fearless Steps Project on LanguageARC. ***(right)***: Explore Apollo Website. ***(right top)***: Landing page for the website provide options to browse to the audio playback section, games section, or the challenge tasks, ***(right bottom)***: An illustration of a single player web-app game on the website where the user has to move up or down to escape the incoming asteroids.

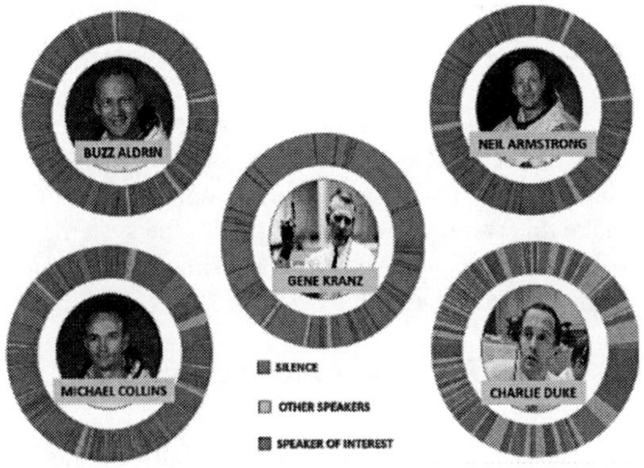

Figure 3: Speaker Duration for Speakers of Interest vs Other MCC Personnel

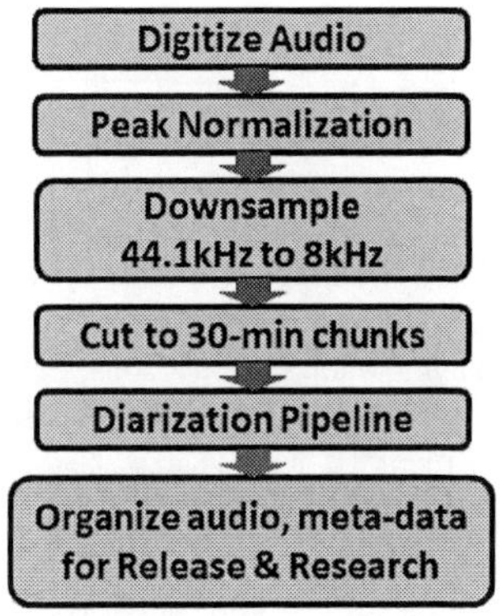

Figure 4: An overview of the steps followed to prepare for distribution of Apollo mission audio data.

recovery efforts, no multi-channel Soundscriber playback units existed to play these tapes. Based on this fact, CRSS estimates that less than 2% of all available audio has ever been heard/recovered since initial recording in the 1960's/70's. A long collaboration between CRSS-UTDallas and NASA engineers/technicians identified one playback system (a second had been dismantled but, eventually, used for parts in the restoration of the other). The original system was modified by CRSS-UTDallas, allowing simultaneous 30-track digitization (Sangwan et al., 2013). The Soundscriber playback system, along with its modifications, can be seen in Fig. 1. This development reduced digitization time by a factor of 30. Digitizing channels simultaneously allowed time synchronization while supporting tape preservation (greatly reducing the stress placed on aging tapes), providing a great resource for both researchers and historians alike.

3.7. The Data Preparation Pipeline

Prior to diarization, digitized audio needs to undergo preprocessing steps. These steps maximize the corpus utility for communities interested in SLT research, historical preservation and team-communication study. The specific steps, described in Fig. 4, were selected to prepare the raw digitized data for diarization process pipeline. Original 44.1 kHz data was preserved separately, and a copy of the data was used for preprocessing to account for future pipeline optimizations. The initial data triage pipeline included moving 17hr digitized channel audio to functional 30min audio chinks with proper filename conventions. New code was developed automatically identify and remove spikes caused due to tapr start and stop. From there, peak normalization was applied and the audio was downsampled to 8kHz (maintaining all relevant information), and cut into uniform 30-minute audio streams, synchronous across all 30 channels on a given tape. These streams are then named as described in Fig. 1, as well as transcribing information gathered from tape heat sheets.

4. FS Challenge Research Corpus

The the FS-APOLLO Corpora is a collection of digitized and largely unlabeled audio data. The fully labelled, multi-functional subset extracted from mission critical phases in the Corpora is referred to as the Fearless Steps Challenge (FSC) Corpus (Joglekar et al., 2020), (Joglekar et al., 2021) (Joglekar et al., 2022).

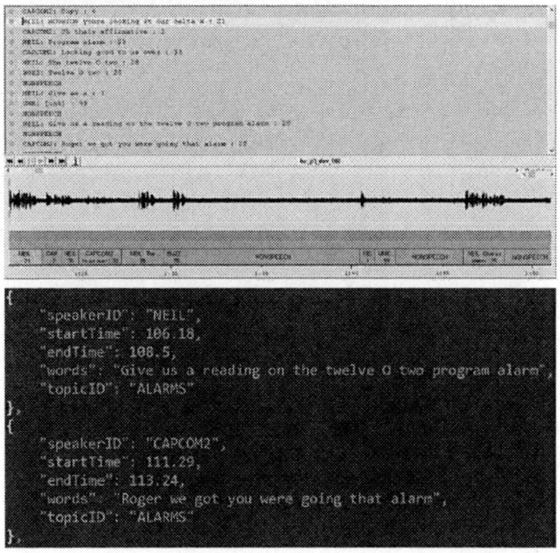

Figure 5: ***(Top)***: Illustration of multi-domain labels in transcriber tool `.trs` format. ***(Bottom)***: Annotations converted to `.json` format for FS challenge phases.

4.1. Fearless Steps Corpora Development

The years 2020 and first half of 2021 were marked by slowly moving digitization efforts due to COVID-19 restrictions. Even with these restrictions, CRSS-UTDallas was able to digitize an additional 50,000 hours of audio. This audio is recorded at 44.1Khz at NASA, JSC which houses the only existing system that can play the Apollo analog tapes. Entire Apollo 8, 9, and 10 were digitized, providing valuable information on MCC speakers. Since the core MCC team remained unchanged over the course of 10 years of the Apollo program, we have a collection of aging-based naturalistic speech corpus which will be developed soon. An illustration of the generated transcriptions are displayed in Fig. 5. The `.trs` files generated by the annotators using the LDC transcriber tool (Cieri and Liberman, 2006) were processed to generate the `.json` files. the Json format was provided to researchers trying to perform speech tasks on continuous audio streams.

4.2. Pipeline Diarization Advancements

The initial system developed in 2017 is a simple DNN with a N-gram language model, with word-error-rate (WER) around 80% on FSC Phase-2 development set. Recently, we further advanced a new baseline system using the advanced hybrid architecture in the Kaldi speech recognition toolkit (Povey et al., 2011). A scenario representation trained in self-supervised manor is incorporated with conventional MFCC and i-vector features to boost the performance on WER (Chen et al., 2021). The results are shown in Table 1.

5. Future Community Resource Direction

CRSS-UTDallas strives towards making continual progress to advance SLT and improve the three FS-APOLLO community resources. Our immediate goals

Table 1: The ASR system is trained on FSC Phase-2 corpus, evaluated on the FSC Phase-4 corpus

Updated Baselines for Fearless Steps Phase-4			
SLT Task	**Metric**	**Dev (%)**	**Eval (%)**
SAD	DCF	4.24	7.57
ASR_track1	WER	28.74	46.3
ASR_track2	WER	24.32	39.4
P2_ASR_track2	WER	26.16	28.9

include promoting self-supervised learning, and releasing over 50,000 hours of the already digitized data to be used for training general representations. We also aim to employ our speaker tracking system 'Finding Waldo' across missions to analyse changes in the speaker traits during the entire duration of the Apollo Program (around 10 years).

6. Conclusion

This study has described the data development, label development, and outreach initiatives conducted so far for the Fearless Steps Apollo Community resource. Naturalistic data development is needed for both technology and scientific / society / historical impact. We aim to make this resource an integral part of the systems that will be developed to learn high-level knowledge directly from speech conversations.

7. Acknowledgements

This project was supported by NSF-CISE Community Resource Project 2016725, and partially by the University of Texas at Dallas from the Distinguished University Chair in Telecommunications Engineering held by J.H.L. Hansen. A special thanks to Katelyn (CRSS-UTDallas Transcription Team) for leading the ground-truth development efforts on the FS Challenge Corpora. Further thanks to the numerous undergraduate senior design students who have contributed to supporting CRSS including Sesank as lead on the preprocessing pipeline and Sapnaben as lead in organizing information from images of digitized tapes.

8. Bibliographical References

Barker, J., Watanabe, S., Vincent, E., and Trmal, J. (2018). The fifth 'chime' speech separation and recognition challenge: Dataset, task and baselines. In *Proc. Interspeech 2018*, pages 1561–1565.

Bengio, Y., Courville, A., and Vincent, P. (2013). Representation learning: A review and new perspectives. *IEEE transactions on pattern analysis and machine intelligence*, 35(8):1798–1828.

Chen, S.-J., Xia, W., and Hansen, J. H. (2021). Scenario aware speech recognition: Advancements for apollo fearless steps & chime-4 corpora. *arXiv preprint arXiv:2109.11086*.

Cieri, C. and Liberman, M. (2006). More data and tools for more languages and research areas: A progress report on ldc activities. In *LREC*, pages 779–782.

Hansen, J. H., Joglekar, A., Shekhar, M. C., Kothapally, V., Yu, C., Kaushik, L., and Sangwan, A. (2019). The 2019 Inaugural Fearless Steps Challenge: A Giant Leap for Naturalistic Audio. In *Proc. Interspeech 2019*, pages 1851–1855.

Harper, M. (2015). The automatic speech recogition in reverberant environments (aspire) challenge. In *2015 IEEE Workshop on Automatic Speech Recognition and Understanding (ASRU)*, pages 547–554. IEEE.

Hinton, G. E., Sejnowski, T. J., Poggio, T. A., et al. (1999). *Unsupervised learning: foundations of neural computation.* MIT press.

Joglekar, A., Hansen, J. H., Shekar, M. C., and Sangwan, A. (2020). FEARLESS STEPS Challenge (FS-2): Supervised Learning with Massive Naturalistic Apollo Data. In *Proc. Interspeech 2020*, pages 2617–2621.

Joglekar, A., Sadjadi, S. O., Chandra-Shekar, M., Cieri, C., and Hansen, J. H. (2021). Fearless Steps Challenge Phase-3 (FSC P3): Advancing SLT for Unseen Channel and Mission Data Across NASA Apollo Audio. In *Proc. Interspeech 2021*, pages 986–990.

Joglekar, A., Chen, S.-J., Chandra-Shekar, M., Belitz, C., Yousefi, M., and Hansen, J. H. (2022). Apollo Fearless Steps: Datasets, Challenge Tasks, and SLT system developments for NASA Apollo Missions Audio. In *Manuscript Submitted to Proc. Interspeech 2022*.

Povey, D., Ghoshal, A., Boulianne, G., Burget, L., Glembek, O., Goel, N., Hannemann, M., Motlicek, P., Qian, Y., Schwarz, P., et al. (2011). The kaldi speech recognition toolkit. In *IEEE 2011 workshop on automatic speech recognition and understanding*, number CONF. IEEE Signal Processing Society.

Sangwan, A., Kaushik, L., Yu, C., Hansen, J. H., and Oard, D. W. (2013). 'houston, we have a solution': using nasa apollo program to advance speech and language processing technology. In *INTERSPEECH*, pages 1135–1139.

Scarselli, F., Gori, M., Tsoi, A. C., Hagenbuchner, M., and Monfardini, G. (2008). The graph neural network model. *IEEE trans. on neural networks*, 20(1):61–80.

Shekar, M. M. C. and Hansen, J. H. (2021). Historical audio search and preservation: "finding waldo" within the fearless steps apollo-11 naturalistic audio corpus. *IEEE Signal Processing Magazine *In Review*.

9. Language Resource References

Carletta, J. (2007). Unleashing the killer corpus: experiences in creating the multi-everything ami meeting corpus. *Language Resources and Evaluation*, 41(2):181–190.

Cieri, C., Graff, D., Kimball, O., Miller, D., and Walker, K. (2004). Fisher english training speech part 1 transcripts. *Philadelphia: Linguistic Data Consortium.*

Hansen, J. H., Sangwan, A., Joglekar, A., Bulut, A. E., Kaushik, L., and Yu, C. (2018). Fearless steps: Apollo-11 corpus advancements for speech technologies from earth to the moon. In *Proc. Interspeech 2018*, pages 2758–2762.

Ryant, N., Church, K., Cieri, C., Cristia, A., Du, J., Ganapathy, S., and Liberman, M. (2018). First dihard challenge evaluation plan.

Creating Mexican Spanish Language Resources through the *Social Service* Program

Carlos Daniel Hernández-Mena, Ivan Vladimir Meza Ruiz
Language and Voice Lab, Instituto de Investigaciones en Matemáticas Aplicadas y en Sistemas
Reykjavik University, Universidad Nacional Autónoma de México
Menntavegur 1, Reykjavík, Z.P. 101, Iceland, Ciudad Universitaria, Mexico City, Mexico, CP. 04510
carlosm@ru.is,ivanvladimir@turing.iimas.unam.mx

Abstract

This work presents the path toward the creation of eight Spoken Language Resources under the umbrella of the Mexican *Social Service* national program. This program asks undergraduate students to donate time and work for the benefit of their society as a requirement to receive their degree. The program has thousands of options for the students who enroll. We show how we created a program which has resulted in the creation of open language resources which now are freely available in different repositories. We estimate that this exercise is equivalent to a budget of more than half a million US dollars. However, since the program is based on retribution from the students to their communities there has not been a necessity of a financial budget.

1. Introduction

In recent times there has been a rise in the number of available Language Resources for different speech processing and NLP tasks (Ray et al., 2018). However, this rise has not been equal for all languages and their variants (Hernández-Mena et al., 2017). The environment for the creation of Language Resources is different among regions and countries. In particular, for Latin America there has been reported a notable gap in the availability of resources among other aspects (Poblete and Pérez, 2020; Sanchez-Pi et al., 2022). In our experience, one of the main obstacles to the creation of resources this region is related to the economy, as research and industry budgets are small. Additionally, with recent ethics recommendations for fair pay, the creation of resources becomes more difficult, although, it is important to notice that fair payment is a necessity in several regions (Shmueli et al., 2021).

In this work, we present our approach to creating Language Resources for the Mexican and Latin American Spanish variants. To tackle the lack of financial resources, we rely on a national and institutionalized social program that every undergraduate has to comply with. This program is known in the region as *social service/Servicio Social*[1] which requires by law that an undergraduate student has to donate 480 hours of activities beneficial to society. In particular, this program encourages students to donate work hours in activities related to their field of study. By creating an option for students of engineering and linguistics, we have been able to collect up to 10 hours of speech per student, which has yielded eight freely available resources that support research in Mexican Spanish.

[1] We use this translation for the name of the program in the absence of a better option. It is not related to the English terms *social services* or *social work*, but may be considered more similar to *community service* or *civic service*.

2. Context of Mexican *Social service*

Social service programs have been implemented around the world (UNESCO, 1984). In Mexico, the *Social Service* was started in 1935 as a requirement to be able to obtain an undergraduate degree in the *Universidad Nacional Autónoma de México* (UNAM). At that time it was the only institution that had such a requirement. By 1945 *Social Service* became a national program which any undergraduate student had to do by law. The main goal of the program was to give back to the society which had financed public education in Mexico and to allow students to acquire experience and practice in their field. In order to reach these goals, students have to apply to a registered option which is associated with a public institution. Once students join they have to donate 480 hours at a maximum rate of 20 hours per week (half time job), which guarantees that they spend at least six months in activities in support of society with a maximum duration of two years. Students have a great variety of options to enroll in. For most of the registered options, the students do not receive financial compensation; however, a few options requiring relocation can provide a scholarship.

3. Design of a *Social service* for Language Resources Creation

In 2013, one of the authors of this work established a *Social service* option for Engineering and Linguistics students at the UNAM's Engineering and Philosophy and Linguistics Faculties. The option was called "Development of Speech Tecnologies" and had the goal of creating speech resources and tools. This option was available for students until 2020 with a gap during 2015.

Since the start of the *Social Service* option, it was clear that this was a good opportunity to focus on activities that facilitated the creation of Language Resources, in particular for speech since there were not many resources that were open and freely available for research

Proceedings of the 2nd Workshop on Novel Incentives in Data Collection from People @LREC2022, pages 20–24

or development. With this in mind, in the registered program students could perform any of the following activities:

Segmentation of audio: In this task students identify utterance segments in long audio recordings. These segments are fine-grained in the sense that they tend to be short (never shorter than 3 seconds). Students were provided with 30 hours of raw recordings and the goal was to have these hours segmented by the end of the *Social Service* commitment period. The recordings could come from sources such as radio-podcasts, talks or readings from books or Wikipedia articles. This task was performed using the *Audacity* software[2]. The software was chosen because it is open source and it was available in different operating systems and platforms.

Speaker-based segmentation: In this case, students identify sequences and segments composed of consecutive turns in which a single speaker speaks. For this task, students were provided with 50 hours of raw recordings to be segmented during the duration of their commitment period. This task was done using the *Audacity* software[3] as well.

Fine-grained speaker segmentation: Based on the segments from the previous task, students refine utterance segments. Since the segments are from a single speaker this is faster than the *Segmentation of audio* task that was done directly on the original recording[4].

Transcription of audio: Students orthographically transcribe what is said in utterance segments. During this task, students were asked to identify errors such as if the recording did not contain speech but another type of sound (e.g., music, background noises, etc). For this task the recommendation was to use the *Notepad++* software[5] which is easy to install and simple enough for the task.

The first year that the option was running, the pipeline consisted of two tasks: *Segmentation* and *transcription of audio*. However, the segmentations produced were not acceptable as they had a large amount of mistakes. The task was harder than originally planned; a student performing the first task of the pipeline will make mistakes at a higher rate than expected. After detecting this large number of errors, the segmentation task was split into two, so the pipeline consisted of three tasks: *Speaker-based segmentation*, *Fine-grained speaker segmentation* and *Transcription of audio*. We discovered there was a better coupling among the segmentations from the new first task and the new second task, since errors in the first task could be detected and fixed during the second one. The complexity of both tasks was less than the original approach because students do not have to worry about the length of segments as they cut, or worry about the order or the content of the recording; they just focus on the quality of the segment and speech.

For the segmentation task, it was important that students had a clear expectation of how the final audio segments should sound. To clarify this, the concept of *clean speech audio* was introduced with the following characteristics:

- There is only one speaker in the segment.
- There shouldn't be music on the background.
- The background noise should be minimal.
- There shouldn't be other types of human-produced sounds such as laughter or applause.

The *Social Service* option started with 3 students but by 2018 there were on average 60 enrolled students per year. The students did not receive any scholarship compensation for their service. However, we believe the popularity of the program derives from the following aspects:

1. The tasks could be performed at home. Although today we are very familiarized with the home-office modality of working, this characteristic was a novelty at the beginning of this option and it soon became very popular among the students. This option was a rarity compared to other options where they could do their *Servicio Social*. This was advantageous for students who lived far from the University or who had a limited amount of time (e.g., they worked to help their families or be able to pay for their studies).

2. The tasks could be done self-paced. At the beginning of the process, the students received a set of recordings that they could work on as it was convenient for them. They could decide their weekly load and schedule and adapt it depending on their availability.

To guarantee a homogeneous quality of the segmentations and transcriptions, students were provided with detailed manuals and some videos that explained the process at the conceptual level and illustrated its stages using the specialized software tools. Beside the instructions on the characteristics of the speech audio, the manuals include instructions about the naming of the files and their ordering in the corresponding folders. Of particular interest was to separate the recordings by

[2]Audacity audio editor website `https://www.audacityteam.org/` (last visited April 2022.)

[3]Idem.

[4]Idem.

[5]Notepad++ editor website: `https://notepad-plus-plus.org/` (last visited April 2022.)

two genders, male and female, and to try to be consistent with the speakers' identities, although the specific identities were discarded in the final version.
In the case of the segmentation task, the manual indicated the desired characteristics of the resulting audios:

- The audio must start and end with a small silence.
- The audio file should have the following format: Microsoft WAV, PCM, 16 bit signed.
- It should be mono (one channel).
- It should have a sampling rate of 16 kHz.
- The filename must include just ASCII characters with underscores between words instead of spaces.

In the case of the transcription task, the students were provided with the following requirements:

- Everything is transcribed in lower case.
- Numbers are transcribed orthographically, not using digits.
- Punctuation marks are not necessary.
- Mispronunciations are recorded in the spelling.
- Foreign words are transcribed as they sound, not with their native spelling.
- Acronyms also are transcribed as they sound.
- Alternative spellings should be avoid, particularly for not well known spellings with double letters, e.g. *clarissa*.
- In case of stuttering register the enunciation of it as much as possible.
- Disfluencies should be registered as sounding, in a short manner and capturing the vocal sound, e.g. *mmm* should be transcribed as *um*, *shhh* as *shu*, etc.
- Novel words should be registered and in case of accentuation (common in Spanish) this should be marked with the acute symbol.

4. Collected resources

There were eight Speech Resources, consisting of ten corpora, created through the *Social Service* option described in this work. All together they consist of 215 hours of speech. The difference between a Speech Resource and corpus is in their publication status; in particular, one Speech Resource could include more than one corpus, as will be shown in one of our speech resources. Table 1 shows the names of the Speech Resources, their size in hours, the year of publication and the repository where they are located. All but one of the resources were published at the Linguistic Data Consortium[6] (LDC) and the other at Open Speech and Language Resources [7] (OSLR).
Seven corpora were developed as part of the CIEMPIESS-UNAM project which was started to create the CIEMPIESS Corpus (Hernández-Mena and Herrera, 2015). The goal was to have a spontaneous speech corpus. It consists of recordings from 43 episodes of broadcast by Radio IUS, a UNAM radio station, with each episode being one hour long. Episodes are comprised of spontaneous conversations between a radio moderator and guests, and their main topic is legal issues. Approximately 78% of the speakers were males, and the rest were females. At a later time, **CIEMPIES Light** (Hernández-Mena and Herrera, 2017) was released, which was an updated and improved CIEMPIESS version but it did not include the automatic phonological transcriptions that the original resources did. This corpus also was designed to be easy to use with Kaldi software (Povey et al., 2011).
A problem with the CIEMPIESS and CIEMPIESS Light corpora was that they are unbalanced, particularly because there are few female speakers. In order to solve this bias, two new resources were created: **CIEMPIESS Balance** (Hernández-Mena, 2018) and **CIEMPIESS experimentation** (Hernández-Mena, 2019a). The first one is the inverse image of the CIEMPIESS corpus (Hernández-Mena and Herrera, 2015) in terms of gender since it contains more speech from female speakers than male. Its goal was that once combined with CIEMPIESS Light, both would produce a gender balanced corpus. On the other hand, the CIEMPEISS Experimentation resource consists of three corpora: *Complementary*, *Fem* and *Test*. These corpora had a specific goal: the *Complementary* corpus consists of a minimal set of utterances to constitute a phonetically balanced corpus; *Fem* consists of the remaining transcriptions of female speakers' recordings that were not included in Balanced; finally, *Test* is a test set of spontaneous speech.
It was during the beginning of the CIEMPIESS-UNAM project that the *Social Service* contributed to the creation of the **CHM150** corpus (Hernández-Mena and Herrera, 2016). This corpus is comprised of Mexican Spanish microphone speech from 75 male and 75 female speakers in a quiet office environment. The speech is spontaneous, triggered by open questions or by requesting the description of a painting shown to the speaker on a computer monitor. Its characteristics make it a candidate to be an evaluation corpus, but it is a challenging corpus since the speech is spontaneous.
Since the series of resources associated with the CIEMPIESS project was spontaneous speech, there

[6]LDC website: `https://catalog.ldc.upenn.edu/` (last visited April 2022.)

[7]OSLR website: `https://openslr.org` (last visited April 2022.)

was an additional effort to create resources around read speech. For this it was decided to use LibriVox[8] (Hernández-Mena, 2020) which collects open and freely available readings of public domain books, and *Wikipedia grabada*[9] (Hernández-Mena and Ruiz, 2021) which is composed of reading recordings from Wikipedia articles.
Finally, the team decided to work on the TEDx collection of talks. For this a new corpus was proposed (Hernández-Mena, 2019b). The speech in this resource is spontaneous; however, there are large monologues which helped with the segmentation of it and to process it in a timely fashion.

Corpus	Size	Published
CIEMPIESS	17h	LDC/2015
CHM150	1.6h	LDC/2016
CIEMPIESS Light	18h	LDC/2017
CIEMPIESS Balance	18h	LDC/2018
CIEMPIESS Experimentation	40h	LDC/2019
TEDx Spanish	24h	OSLR/2019
LibriVox Spanish	73h	LDC/2020
Wikipedia Spanish	25h	LDC/2021

Table 1: Corpora produced by the *Social Service* option described in this work, size given in hours.

5. Ethical concerns

We are aware that there could be concerns that not paying the students is not a fair situation. In fact most of the *Social service* options in Mexico are without payment, and from the legal point of view the law gives that prerogative to the administrator of the *Social Service* option. From the social and ethical point of view, the implicit contract in Mexican society is that students have to give back, particularly in the public system in which students receive a free education. The program is based on a reciprocation principle. In our case the program here described had the goal of not becoming an exploitation case where students work more than what the laws require. To achieve this we implemented the following policies:

- The work load was calculated for 480 hours, and it was constantly validated for the different tasks.
- As mentioned, we provided a maximum flexibility to perform the assigned task. For example, some students did not finish as planned when the 2020 COVID-19 pandemic started, so together with the schools we allowed them to finish their process from one to up to two years after.
- Minimum hardware requirements: the chosen software guaranteed that required computer power was minimal, and no specific brand or OS was necessary. Students had a heterogeneous set of computers and this flexibility allowed them to use their current machines for the work. Also, we did not use online based software since many of them had restricted Internet access.
- To guarantee the impact of the students' work, the created resources were released under an open and freely available license. This was explained to the students at the beginning of the commitment period.

What has to be highlighted about these resources is that there might exist some implicit bias in the work since the segmenter and transcriber population is comprised of undergraduate students. This is something to have in mind since it is the population that the social service program is addressed toward.

6. Conclusion

In this work we describe the use of a *Social Service* option to create Language Resources, in particular for Speech. From our calculations we estimate that the 480 hours invested in this project corresponds approximately to $4,000$ USD, which amounts to an investment of $800,000$ USD when we consider that more than 200 students have enrolled and contributed to the creation of freely and openly available resources. For us, this exemplifies a success story of this approach in which solidarity and retribution from the students allow the collection of large resources of Spoken Mexican Spanish.
As future work we plan to continue working with speech resources, since we need more resources to capture well the richness of the region, particularly for spontaneous speech and multiple speaker scenarios. However, we would like to explore large collaborations based on extended reciprocation principles. For instance, we would like to collaborate with public institutions in which social service is not established but can provide training or scholarships to the students to continue to develop open language resources.

7. Acknowledgements

The authors thank the students of the Social Service option "Desarrollo de Tecnologías del Habla" from the Facultad de Ingeniería (FI) and Facultad de Filosofía y Letras (FFyL) of the Universidad Nacional Autónoma de México (UNAM), we are thankful for all the hard work. The authors also thank Caitlin Laura Richter for her suggestions and comments on the current version of the paper. Carlos Hernández-Mena thanks the support from Language and Voice Lab from Reykjavik University in the realization of this manuscript.

[8]LibriVox website `https://librivox.org/` (last visited April 2022)

[9]Wikipedia *grabada* website `https://es.wikipedia.org/wiki/Wikiproyecto:Wikipedia_grabada` (last visited April 2022)

8. Bibliographical References

Hernández-Mena, C. D., Meza-Ruiz, I. V., and Herrera, A. (2017). Automatic speech recognizers for mexican spanish and its open resources. *Journal of applied research and technology*, 15(3):259–270.

Poblete, B. and Pérez, J. (2020). Minding the ai gap in latam. *Communications of the ACM*, 63(11):61–63.

Povey, D., Ghoshal, A., Boulianne, G., Burget, L., Glembek, O., Goel, N., Hannemann, M., Motlicek, P., Qian, Y., Schwarz, P., Silovsky, J., Stemmer, G., and Vesely, K. (2011). The kaldi speech recognition toolkit. In *IEEE 2011 Workshop on Automatic Speech Recognition and Understanding*. IEEE Signal Processing Society, December. IEEE Catalog No.: CFP11SRW-USB.

Ray, J., Johnny, O., Trovati, M., Sotiriadis, S., and Bessis, N. (2018). The rise of big data science: A survey of techniques, methods and approaches in the field of natural language processing and network theory. *Big Data and Cognitive Computing*, 2(3):22.

Sanchez-Pi, N., Martí, L., Garcia, A. B., Yates, R., Vellasco, M., and Coello, C. (2022). A roadmap for ai in latin america. *PLoS neglected tropical diseases*.

Shmueli, B., Fell, J., Ray, S., and Ku, L.-W. (2021). Beyond fair pay: Ethical implications of nlp crowdsourcing. *arXiv preprint arXiv:2104.10097*.

UNESCO. (1984). El servicio social universitario un instrumento de innovaciÓn en la educaciÓn superior. Technical report, UNESCO.

9. Language Resource References

Carlos Daniel Hernández-Mena and Abel Herrera. (2015). *CIEMPIESS LDC2015S07*. Linguistic Data Consortium, CIEMPIESS-UNAM project, ISLRN 838-468-581-053-6.

Carlos Daniel Hernández-Mena and Abel Herrera. (2016). *CHM150 LDC2016S04*. Linguistic Data Consortium, CIEMPIESS-UNAM project, ISLRN 649-160-209-726-6.

Carlos Daniel Hernández-Mena and Abel Herrera. (2017). *CIEMPIESS Light LDC2017S23*. Linguistic Data Consortium, CIEMPIESS-UNAM project, ISLRN 273-364-546-427-6.

Carlos Daniel Hernández-Mena and Iván Vladimir Meza Ruiz. (2021). *Wikipedia Spanish Speech and Transcripts LDC2021S07*. Linguistic Data Consortium, ISLRN 676-370-775-701-9.

Carlos Daniel Hernández-Mena. (2018). *CIEMPIESS Balance LDC2018S11*. Linguistic Data Consortium, CIEMPIESS-UNAM project, ISLRN 304-456-056-609-5.

Carlos Daniel Hernández-Mena. (2019a). *CIEMPIESS Experimentation LDC2019S07*. Linguistic Data Consortium, CIEMPIESS-UNAM project, ISLRN 139-696-537-175-5.

Carlos Daniel Hernández-Mena. (2019b). *TEDx Spanish Corpus. Audio and transcripts in Spanish taken from the TEDx Talks; shared under the CC BY-NC-ND 4.0 license*.

Carlos Daniel Hernández-Mena. (2020). *LibriVox Spanish LDC2020S01*. Linguistic Data Consortium, ISLRN 256-321-086-598-2.

Fictionary-Based Games for Language Resource Creation

Steinunn Rut Friðriksdóttir, Hafsteinn Einarsson
University of Iceland
Reykjavík, Iceland
{srf2, hafsteinne}@hi.is

Abstract

In this paper, we present a novel approach to data collection for natural language processing (NLP), linguistic research and lexicographic work. Using the parlor game Fictionary as a framework, data can be crowd-sourced in a gamified manner, which carries the potential of faster, cheaper and better data when compared to traditional methods due to the engaging and competitive nature of the game. To improve data quality, the game includes a built-in review process where players review each other's data and evaluate its quality. The paper proposes several games that can be used within this framework, and explains the value of the data generated by their use. These proposals include games that collect named entities along with their corresponding type tags, question-answer pairs, translation pairs and neologism, to name only a few. We are currently working on a digital platform that will host these games in Icelandic but wish to open the discussion around this topic and encourage other researchers to explore their own versions of the proposed games, all of which are language-independent.

Keywords: Games With A Purpose, Language Games, Deception Games, Crowd-Sourcing, Data Collection, Corpus Construction

1. Introduction

Language resources (LRs) are an essential part of natural language processing (NLP), linguistic research and lexicographic work. Recent years have seen a tidal wave of data-driven approaches, increasing the demand for large quantities of annotated data. However, creating these resources is a time-consuming and expensive process which often requires a considerable amount of manual labor. In this paper, we propose a novel method for crowd-sourcing LRs using a Game With A Purpose (GWAP) inspired by a parlor game known as Fictionary[1].

Fictionary is a deception game in which players guess the definition of an obscure word. In each round, one player selects and announces a word from the dictionary, and other players individually compose definitions for it. The made-up definitions, as well as the correct one, are collected blindly by the selector and read aloud, and the players vote on which definition they believe to be correct. Points are awarded for correct guesses, correct definitions, and for having a fake definition guessed by another player. If a player votes for their own guess they do not receive any points. However, they might still do that to deceive other players into voting for that guess as well.

Many games can be formulated within this framework that could be used to create or expand LRs via crowd-sourcing. For example, in a title generation game, players are given the first few lines of a news article and are then asked to guess its title. Subsequently, the players vote for the best title, receiving points when another player votes for their guess. This is where deception comes in as a player might vote for their own answer in order to get others to vote for it as well. The data generated by this game can be used to train a model that generates titles in an extreme summarization fashion or evaluates candidate titles for news articles.

The advantage of our method is that it is relatively quick and inexpensive to generate new LRs using this method if sufficiently many players participate. In addition, our method is potentially more engaging and fun for participants than other methods of data collection. Since the games are structured as competitions, the players are incentivized to create high-quality data as long as the incentives of the competition align with creating quality data. The voting phase of the game, explained in Section 3.3, can help identify good data as the number of votes can be considered a quality indicator. The games can also be customized to target specific languages or domains, making them very versatile.

However, it is important to note that the games must be designed carefully in order to ensure that the players are actually incentivized to create high-quality data. In some cases, players may be more interested in winning the game than in creating high-quality data, which could lead to lower-quality LRs. Therefore, it is important to carefully consider the game design in order to ensure that the players' incentives are aligned with the researcher's goals. Additionally, the data preparation costs (as input to the games) can be significant and would continue to be so if games were ported to new languages and domains.

We are working on a digital game for these types of games in Icelandic but we would like to start a discussion by pointing out this opportunity to other researchers who might be interested in studying this gamified framework of data collection. In this paper, we propose several games that fit within this framework and discuss further aspects of this framework to collect labeled data.

[1] Also known as "The Dictionary Game" along with a boardgame version called Balderdash.

Proceedings of the 2nd Workshop on Novel Incentives in Data Collection from People @LREC2022, pages 25–31
Marseille, 25 June 2022.

2. Literature Review

Data-driven approaches have rapidly gained popularity in the field of natural language processing and with that comes the need for massive LRs. While certain types of data can be mined from various sources such as websites, newspapers and books, manual work is still needed in many cases where specifically annotated data is required. As manual labor can quickly become expensive, crowd-sourcing methods have been used to reduce costs and spread the workload. This can, however, lead to the problem of less engaged workers that quickly tire of their tasks, potentially rendering the data half-finished and thus inusable (Ogawa et al., 2020). Using motivation techniques through gamification, such as earning points or badges and climbing up leaderboards, can significantly increase user engagement and gratification when performing crowd-sourcing tasks.

2.1. Games with a purpose

Deterding et al. refer to gamification as "the use of video game elements in non-gaming systems to improve user experience (UX) and user engagement". Using game heuristics when designing interfaces in non-game services increases participant enjoyment which in turn can raise interest and public participation in a given task (Deterding et al., 2011). While not prominent, the GWAP methodology has been used to collect NLP data for over a decade. In 2008, Chamberlain et al. developed the game Phrase Detectives where players collect anaphoric information in a gamified environment. The game Zombilingo, proposed by Fort et al. in 2014, uses several motivation techniques in order to incentivize players to create dependecy syntax data for French. In the same year, Jurgens and Navigli proposed an annotation paradigm that asks users to create a mapping from WordNet senses to images and perform word sense disambiguation while playing graphical video games.

In 2020, Araneta et al. introduced Substituto, a language learning game designed for English L2 learners that simultaneously crowd-sources NLP data. In 2021, Arhar Holdt et al. presented Game of Words, a gamified mobile application where users were encouraged to improve and enhance two automatically compiled Slovene dictionaries. In the same year, Eryiğit et al introduced a gamified approach to compiling an idiom corpora in Turkish and Italian. They designed a Telegram messaging bot that serves as a multiplayer game for native speakers that compete with each other while creating ideomatic and non-ideomatic sentences and rating each other's propositions. Users were additionally incentivized using gift cards (Eryiğit et al., 2021).

2.2. Crowd-sourcing projects in Iceland

The Common Voice project is a multilingual crowd-sourcing initiative where participants are asked to record their voice by reading sentences that they are presented with on the screen, and other participants are subsequently asked to verify the recordings using a simple voting system (Ardila et al., 2020). In July 2020, it was reported that the corpus had reached over 7,000 hours of voice data in over 50 languages. The Icelandic version of the project has used gamification in their marketing to great success. In 2022, 118 elementary schools competed for a prize where the goal was to read as many sentences as possible for the project. This has been an annual event since 2019 and has resulted in 1.5 million voice samples being collected for the project[2]. Additionally, over 360,000 voice samples were collected in a similar contest between Icelandic organizations and companies.

In 2021, Jasonarson used gamification and crowd-sourcing in order to collect LRs in Icelandic. His website, Málfróði (e. *linguistically knowledgeable* but in the form of a masculine name), incentivizes players to rate data according to their formality and inappropriateness on the one hand, and evaluate their linguistic correctness (spelling and grammar) according to their own conviction on the other hand. The players receive points for each submission they make. They receive more points if their submission is marked by the other players as having good quality, and they receive maximum points if their submission gets points from the majority of other players, indicating that their submission is reflective of public consensus (Jasonarson, 2021).

In 2021, Snæbjarnarson et al. published a resource where they present their extractive question answering (QA) dataset for Icelandic (Snæbjarnarson et al., 2021). Following the lead of Clark et al. (2020), they asked human annotators to write questions inspired by a 100-character-long prompt from Icelandic Wikipedia articles, but to make sure that the prompt did not answer their questions. In a second phase, the participants were asked to answer each other's questions. Based on that approach a mobile game was developed to build a larger crowd-sourced dataset for Icelandic[3]. The task was presented as a mobile game where users collect points and can receive prices based on their scores.

3. General game framework

In this section, we define the game and emphasize variations of it. The game is played over a predetermined number of rounds and the goal of each player is to maximize their points. We show an example of a game round in a title generation game in Figure 1.

3.1. Preparation phase

The round starts with the players receiving the same task. The task can come with a side-objective. For example, in a title generation game the side objective

[2]Scoreboard for elementary schools in Iceland: `https://samromur.is/grunnskolakeppni2022`.

[3]Available at `http://www.spurningar.is`

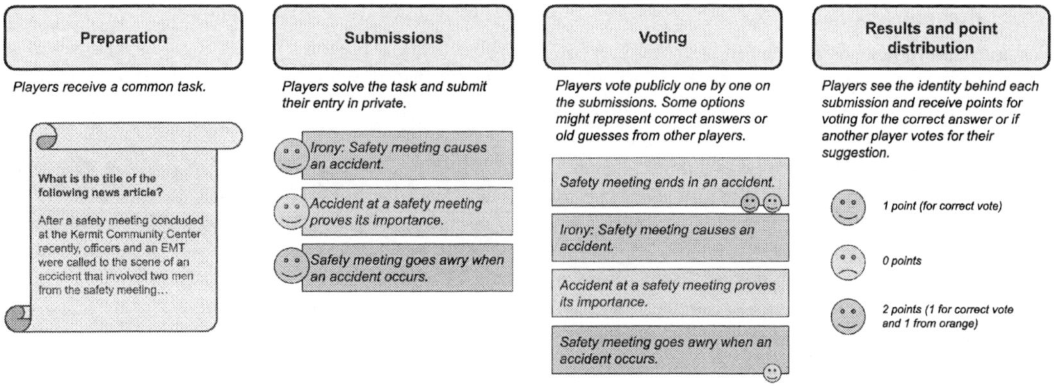

Figure 1: Example of a round in a title generation game. The players are presented with a task and everyone writes their solution that they submit in a private manner. After everyone has submitted their entry they proceed to a voting round. In a voting round, additional options might be available such as a correct title (green) in this case, or possibly old submissions from external players for the same task (not shown). The players vote for what option they think is correct in this case (or the one they like the most with respect to a given objective in case a correct option is not available). Finally, players receive points based on the voting result and the identity behind each submitted item is revealed.

could be to write a short or witty title. Such side objectives can serve as additional labels for data generated by the players in that round.

3.2. Submission phase

Each player writes a submission in private for the given task. This phase can be played with a timer if the players are playing in real-time or without a timer if the players are ready to spend time on their submissions and play asynchronously.

An asynchronous approach can be implemented in a manner similar to a popular game called Wordle where each day the participants play a single round and need to vote before tha day ends.

3.3. Voting phase

After all players have submitted their entry they proceed to a voting phase. The players can either vote publicly one by one or they can all vote simultaneously. There is a qualitative difference between these two approaches because if players vote one by one then their vote can influence the decision of the next players in line. This presents an opportunity for deception where a player might vote for their own submission in order to deceive the other players into voting for it as well.

The options available in the voting phase do not necessarily need to consist only of the submissions of the players. They can also include a correct answer (if one is available) or old submissions made by external players for the same task. When the number of options is greater than the number of players it can be sensible to give players more than a single vote to increase the chances of them receiving points in the round and even allow them to vote for the same item more than once. This could further affect the point calculation, for example, by doubling the number of points a player assigned to a correct item.

We note that a digital experience also presents more opportunities for labeling. In the voting phase, players could also be presented with the option to assign additional labels to the submissions that do not award points. For example, they could tag submissions with emojis or some fixed reactions that are there to drive engagement in the game but could serve as interesting labels as well.

3.4. Results phase

The identity behind each suggestion is revealed and players receive points based on the votes in the results phase. A player receives points when another player voted for their suggestion. When a correct option is available the players also receive points for voting for it.

After this phase, the game proceeds to the next round.

3.5. Single player variant

In a single player variant of the game the player skips the submission phase and proceeds directly to the voting phase, where they are presented with several items. In case of a correct item, the aim of the player is to spot it. When a correct item is not available the aim of the player is to spot the most popular item where the popularity of an item is determined by its past success. This approach also allows for a more passive participation as this type of voting could be done at any given moment, serving more as a validation of previously generated data.

3.6. Target users

We note that the game could be implemented, for example, in the form of an app for mobile phones and tablets or as a website. On an accessible digital platform, the game can be played by a broad group of users. However, some of the games might be more relevant to a classroom environment where the aim is to have students learn about e.g. domain-specific vocabulary in a game that closely resembles the original Fictionary.
With a sufficiently general platform the user could define tasks themselves. This can be beneficial for teachers who want to use this method in their classroom to engage students in a novel manner.

3.7. Data logging

For a game built using this framework, it is necessary to log the configuration of each game session along with the data generated in that session. Such logging helps researchers filter out data that was not generated in a particular manner. For example, if players are given a choice between voting simultaneously or one by one when a game session is started then that choice should be recorded such that one could select data from sessions where everyone voted simultaneously.

4. Game suggestions

In this section, we present several ideas for games that could be used for data collection, particularly for NLP. We further suggest the usability of the data collected for each game.

4.1. Summarization

In a title generation game, players receive the first few paragraphs of a news article and are asked to generate a title for it. The players are then asked to vote for the best title. Points can be awarded based on a majority vote or such that each player receives points when another player votes for their submission. Creating a good source dataset for a game of this type does not require significant work given the amount of publicly available news articles.
The resulting dataset could be used to train a model to evaluate candidate titles for a news article. A model could also be used to generate titles in an extreme summarization fashion. We believe that this game has the potential to be engaging for players since they have the opportunity to come up with witty and clever title suggestions. Additional objectives can also be provided to the players if the aim is to create serious titles, funny titles, short titles, long titles et cetera.

4.2. Word sense disambiguation

In this game the aim is to create a new data set for word sense disambiguation. Players would be given a sentence with a word highlighted, and would need to write a definition of that word. Points could be given in a similar manner to the original game where the player who provides the correct definition gets a point as well as the player whose definition is voted for by the other players, regardless of truth value. This game can be considered a generalization of Fictionary since the word is given with the addition of surrounding context. If the examples are hard, then the players will generally be wrong and the value of the data might appear less clear than for other game suggestions. However, we note that wrong suggestions that are good in deceiving players could be used as negative examples when training a model for word sense disambiguation or as a test set to get a better measure of the performance of word sense disambiguation models.

4.3. Question answering and generation

In this game, the goal is to generate new data for question answering systems. Players would be given a question and would need to write an answer for that question. Points could be given as in the previous game where players that provide the correct answer get points as well as the players who manage to deceive other players into voting for their answers. The game can also be reversed where players are given an answer and have to write an appropriate question based on some additional requirements such as the question needing to be serious, witty or sounding like a riddle.

4.4. Paraphrasing

In this game, the aim is to generate paraphrases for a given sentence in a particular style. Players would be given a sentence and an objective and would need to write a paraphrase for that sentence while trying to satisfy the objective. The objective could be stylistic, e.g., to make the sentence more serious or more funny. The objective could also be to make the sentence shorter, longer or simpler.
Data from a paraphrasing game could be useful for training paraphrasing models that can change the style of a given text. It could also aid in training models with the aim of making text simpler to read and more accessible, e.g. for people with disabilities or L2 learners.

4.5. Generating NER data

In this game the aim is to generate new Named Entity Recognition data. Players would be given a sentence with some words replaced by blanks. The players would need to fill in the blanks with named entities that satisfy a given tag, e.g. person, location or organization. The task can also come with an objective, such as finding entities that make the sentence funny while still satisfying the objective. The task can also be flipped, i.e., the players receive some fixed entities and their task is to write a sentence involving said entities, possibly with some side objective as before.
The resulting data of entities, in context, labeled with their NER tags can be used to train NER models. The task for fixed entities could be especially useful for generating training data for entities that occur rarely in text.

4.6. Poem games

4.6.1. Finishing poems

In a poem finishing game, players receive the first few lines of a poem and are asked to finish it with respect to a given rhyme scheme. This is a variation of a game that was (and still is, on special occasions) commonly played in Iceland, usually between two players that took turns finishing each other's poems. The objective of the original game is usually to be witty or pointed towards the opponent, an element that could easily be adapted into the voting system. A point-scale could even be added (using emojis, for instance) where the players rank the proposed lines based on their wittiness. The resulting dataset could be used to train a poem generator. Such a generator could be a good source of inspiration for song and story writers as well as being interesting on its own: what type of poems does an AI write?

4.6.2. Writing poems for a given subject

In this game, players receive a given context (for example, a news article) and are required to write a poem with respect to a given rhyme scheme that reflects its contents. The objective could be similar to that of the previous game, that is, to make the poem particularly witty, sarcastic or pointed with ranked scores.

The resulting dataset could be used to train an abstractive summarization model whose output is in the form of a poem. We are not aware of models that perform this type of summarization although we speculate that large generative language models might have such capabilities at some point.

4.7. Story writing

4.7.1. Story by a committee

In a story game, players start with a blank prompt or some general objective, and everyone writes the beginning of a story. The players then vote on the suggestions and the winner becomes the prompt for the next round where the process is repeated until the story ends. This way, the players collectively write a story about a given subject. Alternatively, the game could be played in turns where each player has a specific amount of time to write their prompts, skipping the voting until the end where a player could be voted as being the most creative or the funniest contributor. The advantage of this approach is that it does not require any data to get started. As an objective the players could be given a list of characters, settings, and objects, and then have to come up with a story that includes all of those elements.

The disadvantage of this approach is that the players might take a lot of time to write and each game round is not independent of the rounds that came before. This might lead to lower engagement than with the other games but it could still be used in a proper setting, for example, as an exercise in a class on writing short-stories. Additionally, as a single-player mode, a computer player such as GPT-3 could be used as an opponent, giving the player an instant response.

4.7.2. Natural language dialogues

In this game the aim is to generate natural dialogue. Players would take on the role of characters in a dialogue and would need to continue a conversation. In any given round, everyone responds on behalf of the same character and the players vote which response will be chosen to continue the dialogue. This type of game could be used in a teaching setting, particularly with L2 learners which in turn would collect a language variant that is often underrepresented in textual data.

The data generated from a game like this one could be used to generate training data for a chat bot. If the users are given additional instructions then that information can be used for finer-grained dialogue tasks. For example, if users are instructed to be rude, then the data could be used to train a rudeness detection model.

A game of this type could also be an interesting exercise for students writing scenes in a play in a democratic manner. In this process, everyone can collectively decide on how to move a dialogue forward without the risk of a single individual taking over the process.

4.8. Machine translation

4.8.1. Translations of technical terms

A game could be designed to generate suggestions for translations of technical terms and domain-specific words. Players would be given a foreign word along with its definition and would need to suggest a translation, which could in principle be a neologism. The suggestions could then be voted on by other players, scoring the suggestor of the winning candidate points on the leaderboard.

Creating suggestions in this manner could help committees and professional translators settle faster on good translations for new technical terms.

4.8.2. Translating sentences

In this game, the players receive a sentence they need to translate into a given language. This can be played as a language learning game where a group helps each other learn a new language, similar to an online tandem partner. But for native speakers of a given language, the game could lead to high-quality paired training examples. Since players would suggest many possible translations and one might not obviously be the best one, it might be better to let the players rate each translation in this game than to vote for a single one.

4.8.3. Sentences from fixed words

In this game, players are given a list of words and need to write sentences that include those words. The sentences could be evaluated by the other players based on different factors, such as grammar, fluency, and appropriateness. This is particularly suitable in an L2 learning setting where the list of words can even be given in the players' native language but the players must use them in their target language.

4.9. Neologism

In this game, players are asked to come up with synonyms or definitions for already existing words. A particular objective could be to create words in a certain style or register (e.g. for academia, slang, or for a specific, potentially made-up, dialect). Players could also be asked to invent new words that convey a certain proposed meaning. Players would then vote for the suggestions using a scale and receive points based on their rank. In this game, the focus would be on creativity rather than accuracy.

As with the game proposed in Section 4.8.1, the data generated by this game could be used when coming up with neologisms and translations for new vocabulary entering the language.

4.10. Recipe generator

In this game, players are given a list of ingredients and have to come up with a dish that contains those ingredients. Certain criteria could be introduced as variants of the game, e.g. to create the best vegan recipe or make the highest-calorie or most frugal meal possible from the list of ingredients. Players then vote for the recipe that they like best, scoring the author points on the leaderboard. This data could be used to train a model whose objective is to automatically retrieve recipes from a list of proposed ingredients, which people could then use to get new ideas based on what they currently have in their kitchen. Since a game like this could be challenging for novices it is crucial to record the cooking skill level of each user beforehand.

5. Competition to improve labels

The data acquisition approach we have presented has several interesting qualities when compared to other approaches. First of all, players can be incentivized to create high-quality data since their examples are reviewed by other players. Second, we note that the voting phase of the game can provide interesting information on the quality of the players' entries. Such information could be helpful to train models to rank examples with respect to a given task description. For a title generation game, the model would receive as input the task description as well as the players' entries. The output of the model would then be a score for each entry that can be used to rank which candidate fits best. To get a better estimate of the quality of an entry, it can be used in another round with different players. Players could then be voting not only on their own entries but also on entries submitted by external players. Under such conditions, it could make sense to give the players more than just a single vote since otherwise it might be more challenging for them to get any points at all.

Additionally, each game could start with the instigator configuring which game type they want to play first, what type of voting system they want to use, whether or not they only wish to participate in the voting etc. This metadata would be logged, making it possible to filter out language resources that are created in some specific way.

6. Testing the idea

As a proof of concept, and a qualitative evaluation, we played some of the games proposed in Section 4 with a few collegues. As our platform is not ready, the games were played on paper but in essence they were the same as they would be in a computerized form. None of our collegues had played Fictionary before but they agreed that the framework had the potential to work well. They compared the idea to Kahoot (Dellos, 2015) or Jackbox [4] and mentioned that well designed graphics and music could do a lot for making the game more appealing to users. They agreed that some games were more interesting than others and could be played for entertainment purposes but others resembled a traditional crowd-sourcing task that would quickly get boring. They mentioned that all of the games that involved a side task such as making the answer funny would work well and compared those games in particular to Jackbox. They additionally mentioned that games that involve a single correct answer could be played for entertainment if presented as a trivia game that allows users to level up, collect badges or climb up leaderboards.

When asked whether they would be more likely to play the games if they would be preceded with an explaination regarding their importance for data collection for Icelandic NLP tasks, one of our collegues pointed out that the platform could be presented in two seperate ways. If the idea was to appeal to the masses and get the average user to play, the entertainment value would always be the selling point and the idea of unpayed labour might even put some users off. On the other hand, the platform could be presented in schools as a learning instrument as well as having the higher purpose of helping advance Icelandic to the digital age. Our collegue had played Kahoot in school before and mentioned that the diversion from traditional teaching methods was highly appreciated by the students. They added that if the tasks were presented as a multiple choice, the students' input could provide additional information to train language models. Wrong answers that receive a lot of votes from students would be labelled as particularly hard and could be used as challenging negative examples for language models.

7. Discussion

We have presented a new framework for building LRs in a gamified manner. We have demonstrated several tasks that fit within this framework and which could potentially lead to voluntary participation or participation as an exercise in a classroom environment.

[4] `http://jackboxgames.com`

The key factor which determines the success of this LR generation strategy is how engaging the game turns out to be. An engaging game has the potential to be entertaining for users while simultaneously creating high-quality LRs. Given the success of games such as Balderdash, which have been sold in millions of copies, we believe that this approach has great promise.

We must acknowledge that some games might not be as engaging as others and it is likely not possible to fit every dataset creation task into this format. As an example, a task more challenging than extreme summarization would be to write a summary of the news article that is longer than a single sentence. That is a more tedious task than title generation and possibly less engaging for that reason. One approach to make tasks like this more engaging for the user could be to mix the tasks up so that they are randomly sampled from the set of available games. In case users get bored of a particular task, each round could start with a majority vote where users can vote on whether to cancel or continue with the currently proposed game. Having a good variety of tasks can potentially increase the sense of novelty, which can further drive engagement. The framework could, in principle, also potentially be used for traditional crowd-sourcing tasks where the objective is simply to generate data, without regards to the entertainment value or even scoring points.

Finally, we want to acknowledge that this LR creation process can introduce new biases into a dataset. Dynamics that arise due to the competitive nature of this approach might lead to submissions that are not representative of data acquired through other means. Studying the extent of such a bias remains an open problem and can further help to understand the value of this approach for creating LRs.

8. Acknowledgements

We would like to thank the reviewers for helpful comments on the first submission of this manuscript and our colleagues who helped us playtest the framework.

9. Bibliographical References

Ardila, R., Branson, M., Davis, K., Kohler, M., Meyer, J., Henretty, M., Morais, R., Saunders, L., Tyers, F., and Weber, G. (2020). Common voice: A massively-multilingual speech corpus. In *Proceedings of the 12th Language Resources and Evaluation Conference*, pages 4218–4222, Marseille, France, May. European Language Resources Association.

Arhar Holdt, Š., Logar, N., Pori, E., and Kosem, I. (2021). "game of words": Play the game, clean the database. *EURALEX XIX*.

Chamberlain, J., Poesio, M., Kruschwitz, U., et al. (2008). Phrase detectives: A web-based collaborative annotation game. In *Proceedings of the International Conference on Semantic Systems (I-Semantics' 08)*, pages 42–49.

Clark, J. H., Choi, E., Collins, M., Garrette, D., Kwiatkowski, T., Nikolaev, V., and Palomaki, J. (2020). Tydi qa: A benchmark for information-seeking question answering in typologically diverse languages. *Transactions of the Association for Computational Linguistics*, 8:454–470.

Dellos, R. (2015). Kahoot! a digital game resource for learning. *International Journal of Instructional technology and distance learning*, 12(4):49–52.

Deterding, S., Sicart, M., Nacke, L., O'Hara, K., and Dixon, D. (2011). Gamification. using game-design elements in non-gaming contexts. In *CHI'11 extended abstracts on human factors in computing systems*, pages 2425–2428.

Eryiğit, G., Şentaş, A., and Monti, J. (2021). Gamified crowdsourcing for idiom corpora construction. *Natural Language Engineering*, pages 1–33.

Fort, K., Guillaume, B., and Chastant, H. (2014). Creating zombilingo, a game with a purpose for dependency syntax annotation. In *Proceedings of the First International Workshop on Gamification for Information Retrieval*, pages 2–6.

Grace Araneta, M., Eryigit, G., König, A., Lee, J.-U., Luís, A., Lyding, V., Nicolas, L., Rodosthenous, C., and Sangati, F. (2020). Substituto-a synchronous educational language game for simultaneous teaching and crowdsourcing.

Jasonarson, A. (2021). Málfróði: Að nota lýðvirkjun og leikjavæðingu til að afla gagna fyrir íslenska tungu.

Jurgens, D. and Navigli, R. (2014). It's all fun and games until someone annotates: Video games with a purpose for linguistic annotation. *Transactions of the Association for Computational Linguistics*, 2:449–464.

Ogawa, H., Nishikawa, H., Tokunaga, T., and Yokono, H. (2020). Gamification platform for collecting task-oriented dialogue data. In *Proceedings of the 12th Language Resources and Evaluation Conference*, pages 7084–7093.

10. Language Resource References

Snæbjarnarson, Vésteinn and Einarsson, Bergur Tareq Tamimi and Auðunardóttir, Ingibjörg Iða and Sæmundsson, Unnar Ingi and Bjarnadóttir, Hildur and Gunnarsson, Helgi Valur and Einarsson, Hafsteinn. (2021). *NQiI - Natural Questions In Icelandic - v1.0*.

Using Mixed Incentives to Document Xi'an Guanzhong

Juhong Zhan*, Yue Jiang*, Christopher Cieri†, Mark Liberman†, Jiahong Yuan✱, Yiya Chen★, Odette Scharenborg‡

*Xi'an Jiaotong University, †University of Pennsylvania, Linguistic Data Consortium,
✱Baidu Research, ★Leiden University, ‡Delft University of Technology
{Corresponding Author: ccieri@ldc.upenn.edu}

Abstract

This paper describes our use of mixed incentives and the citizen science portal LanguageARC to prepare, collect and quality control a large corpus of object namings for the purpose of providing speech data to document the under-represented Guanzhong dialect of Chinese spoken in the Shaanxi province in the environs of Xi'an.

Keywords: under-resourced languages, language resources, linguistic data, annotation, novel incentives

1. Introduction

The impetus for this effort was the intersection of interests among the authors: 1) to document the Guanzhong dialect, 2) to develop low-cost, portable, scalable, and replicable language resource development methodologies, 3) to augment the supply of language resources through the use of novel incentives and 4) to innovate human, automated and hybrid methods for rapid documentation of under-resourced languages. This paper describes the Guanzhong dialect, prior efforts to create language resources to study this variety, the research goals of the current collection, the use of a citizen science platform and its implications, recruitment, incentives, collection, quality control and the resulting data.

2. Xi'an Guanzhong

A prior successful collaboration between the Xi'an Jiaotong University and the Linguistic Data Consortium, described in §3, that has resulted in published language resources (Jiang, et al. 2020), encouraged us to continue and expand the collaboration focusing on the Guanzhong dialect spoken in and around Xi'an.

2.1 Background

The Guanzhong dialect of Mandarin (hereafter Guanzhong dialect), also known as Qin language, is a dialect family spoken in the Guanzhong region of Shaanxi Province. The Guanzhong region includes five major cities: Xi'an, Baoji, Xianyang, Weinan, Tongchuan and the Yangling district. Based on the Saanxi Statistical Report (2021), the region has a total area of 55,623 square kilometers and a population of 25,875,539. The Guanzhong dialects can be classified into two sub-dialect groups: the East-fu dialect, spoken in Xián and cities to its east, and West-fu dialect, spoken in e.g. Baoji and regions to the west of Xian (Li, 1989). With an estimated more than 50,000,000 speakers, it ranks among the top 40 languages, above e.g. Polish and Yoruba, in terms of the total number of speakers.

The Guanzhong dialect was once the official language of the Zhou, Qin, Han and Tang dynasties in Chinese history, and in ancient times it was called "Yayan", or the "elegant dialect".

Xi'an is the place where the Guanzhong dialect originated and developed through history. It is the central area of Guanzhong Plain and also the capital city of Shaanxi Province. Known as Chang'an, China's capital during the Tang dynasty. It was authorized by the UNESCO as a world-famous historic city in 1981. Xi'an has served as an imperial capital since ancient times and lasted through thirteen dynasties, roughly two thousand years. Chinese culture, language and writing were all formed and developed during this period.

Deeply rooted in the traditional culture of Xi'an, the Guanzhong dialect has a relatively long history and enjoys a large number of native speakers. Many ancient dialect words still remain in the Guanzhong dialect (Zhao, 2020). The traditional Shaanxi Local opera Qinqiang is sung in the Guanzhong dialect, too.

Documentation of the Guanzhong dialect dates at least to the Han dynasty in the first century BCE with Yang Xiong's development of the *Fangyan* dictionary of regional varieties. Bai (1954) produced a more recent survey of Guanzhong dialects. Current research on the Guanzhong dialect focuses mainly on phonological variations (Wang, 1995, Zhang, 2005), use of special words (Li, 2014) and personal pronouns (Sun, 2021). Despite the long tradition among Sinologists of studying the Guanzhong dialect, it has received less attention than might be expected given the number of speakers. So far, no general purpose speech corpus of Guanzhong dialect has been built, although Xing (2014) proposed the necessity of building a large dialect speech corpus.

2.2 Phonological Characteristics

Lexical tones in Guanzhong Mandarin dialects seem to have quite systematic correspondences to tones in Standard Chinese. In some varieties, the following mappings apply:

1. Yinping (the first or level tone) changes to Qingsheng (the fifth or Neutral tone) (Lu, 2010); for example shēng chǎn is sheng chàn in the Guanzhong dialect.
2. Shangsheng (the third or falling-rising tone) changes to Qusheng (the fourth or falling tone); lǐ jiě is lì jiè in the dialect.

Proceedings of the 2nd Workshop on Novel Incentives in Data Collection from People @LREC2022, pages 32–37
Marseille, 25 June 2022.

3. Qusheng (the fourth or falling tone) changes to Yinping (the first or level tone); for example, wén jiàn is wén jiān in dialect.
4. Yangping (the second or rising tone) remains the same (Zhao, 2017). The dialectal tone of liáng pí is the same as that in Mandarin.

Liu et al. (2020) have also provided a detailed acoustic study of the tonal mapping between Xi'an Mandarin and Standard Chinese.

2.3 Lexical Characteristics

The lexical system is an important aspect of the uniqueness of the Guanzhong dialect (Li, 2014). According to current research findings, in the Guanzhong lexicon, 21.3% of the words are typically dialectal and the remaining 78.7% are consistent with or close to Mandarin (Wang, 2015). The Guanzhong dialect contains complex lexical variations in different aspects, such as pronouns, indicative pronouns, modal particle and so on (Zhao, 2020).

There are a great number of variations in the use of parts of speech. Hóu (monkey) is a noun in Standard Mandarin, but is also used as an adjective in Guanzhong dialect. For example, people could say "Zhè (this) Wā (kid) Hóu (monkey) di (得, an auxiliary word) Taī (very)" which means "this kid is overactive and naughty". The word Chè (Chě in Mandarin) is a verb meaning "tear". In Guanzhong Dialect, it can be used as an adjective in sentence like "Kū zi Chè le", which means the trousers are torn.

3. Prior Corpus Efforts

Several of the authors had collaborated previously to begin creating corpora for the Guanzhong dialect, initially within the *Global TIMIT* framework. Global TIMIT aims to create corpora in multiple languages that share key features with the original TIMIT Acoustic-Phonetic Continuous Speech Corpus (Garofalo et al., 1993), designed to also support the development of speech to text systems. These key features included:

- many speakers
- many fluently-read sentences containing a representative sample of linguistic patterns
- time-aligned lexical and phonetic transcripts
- three classes of sentences according to whether they were read by all speakers, a few speakers, or just one speaker

Global TIMIT differs from the original in features that have proven expensive to implement or not strictly necessary or both. Specifically, while the original TIMIT had a large number of speakers (600) read a relatively small number (10) of sentences each, Global TIMIT reduces the recruiting effort needed to acquire an equivalent volume of data by eliciting 120 sentences from 50 speakers. In addition, Global TIMIT does not require that phonetically rich or balanced or representative sentences are created for each language as were the Harvard Sentences read in the original TIMIT. Rather, corpus designers typically select sentences of reasonable length from existing open sources (e.g. Wikipedia, lists of proverbs, etc.) that they subsequently filter to remove sentences that contain foreign or unusual words or would be otherwise difficult to read fluently. Such filtering can include selecting for phonetic balance or representativeness from this naturally occurring text.

The Linguistic Data Consortium and Xi'an Jiaotong University used the Global TIMIT methodology to create the Mandarin Chinese - Guanzhong Dialect corpus (Jiang et al., 2020) consisting of ~five hours of read speech and transcripts. 3220 sentences were selected from the Chinese Gigaword Fifth Edition (LDC2011T13) corpus of news text. 25 females and 25 males who spoke the Guanzhong dialect each read 120 sentences where 20 sentences were read by all speakers, 40 sentences were read by 10 speakers, and 60 sentences were read by one speaker.

The corpus was recorded in a quiet room at Xi'an Jiaotong University, Xi'an, China. The collection yielded 5999 utterances (one missing). Each utterance appears in its own audio file and is accompanied by time aligned transcripts for each word, phone and tone segment as well as Praat TextGrids.

4. Collection Protocol: Object Naming

The next (i.e. current) data collection, changed a number of parameters to address details of the language that were not the focus of our previous effort. As noted above, two of the most striking differences between the Guanzhong dialect and Standard Mandarin are in the tonal system and lexicon. Speech elicitation through the reading of previously written sentences would be expected to produce data suitable for the study of phonetic and phonological differences, at least to the extent that native speakers produce such differences in read speech. However, in order to gather data on variation in the lexicon, we would need a task in which the contributors were freer to make their own lexical choices. After considering both picture description and object naming, we settled on the latter which would also yield also a picture/speech database that can be used to build visually-grounded speech models (Scholten, Merkx, Scharenborg, 2021). Initial targets were 200 objects named by 20 speakers each.

We then considered gathering images to match the items in the Communicative Development Inventories adapted for Mandarin (Tardif and Fletcher 2008) but decided to use MultiPic "a standardized set of 750 drawings with norms for six European languages" (Duñabeitia et al. 2018) and ongoing effort collecting written namings in additional languages including Chinese (Duñabeitia, p.c.). MutiPic's set of consistently composed colored line drawings saved us the effort of identifying images to use in the object naming but, of course, required adaptation for Guanzhong dialect speakers.

4.1 LanguageARC for Collection and Annotation

The requirements for a platform to collect judgements concerning the appropriateness of the MultiPic images – and eventually for the speech samples themselves – were several. The platform would need to perform adequately in multiple locations in the USA, Netherlands and China where members of the team were located. It would need to be able to collect multiple choice, unconstrained text and speech and accept and display text in Roman and Chinese characters. It should also allow project managers to restrict access to different tasks within the project to different sets of users. Ease of use for project managers and contributors, and the ability to rapidly prototype tasks were important considerations for this somewhat innovative effort. Finally, as the project, from initial conception to the release of the data, took place during the COVID-19 epoch, we could not ask participants to visit a carefully instrumented lab. Instead the platform needed to support entirely remote operation. After considering some alternatives, we prototyped the collection of multiple choice judgements and unconstrained text and speech in the LanguageARC citizen science portal (Cieri and Fiumara, 2020) where performance was sufficient to proceed.

4.2 Image Selection

As above the MultiPic corpus offers us a large number of images that had been normed across multiple European languages. However, it had not yet been adapted for potential contributors living in China. We had anticipated that images of the following types might prove confusing to some speakers:

1. complex images where it's not clear what should be named (#22, a campsite with multiple tents, trees, hills)
2. images specific to a time, place or domain that might not be generally known (#051, a gallows)
3. images that use a 'visual language of deixis' that might not be obvious to users when they first encounter them but may be learned over time (#3, a step on a staircase is shaded) leading to variation across the collection

To select images suitable for presentation in an object naming task to a large number of native Chinese speakers, we first presented each image to a single native speaker of Chinese, living in China, to judge whether others would be able to name the object consistently. Figure 2 shows the LanguageARC task used to present images to and collect judgements from the annotator.

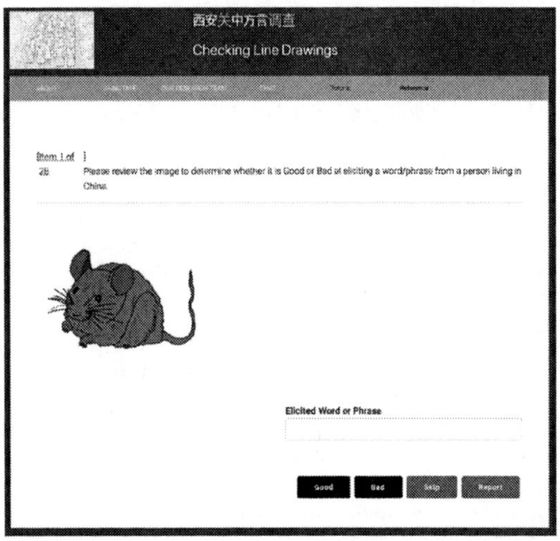

Figure 2: Selecting Appropriate Images

The annotator provided both a judgement as to appropriateness and one or more written labels for the image. A member of the project team, with similar linguistic and cultural background, plus an understanding of our research goals, using the LanguageARC task displayed in Figure 1, reviewed those cases where the annotator expressed uncertainty and made final decisions as to whether the images would be included.

Figure 1: Double Checking Uncertain Judgements

After these two passes, we had identified 622 of the 750 MultiPic images that we believed would easily elicit object namings from Chinese contributors. Most of the excluded images were complex (103, art gallery), tightly connected to Western culture (144, toreador), religion (742, pope) or mythology (184, witch and cauldron) or perhaps just embarrassing (65, buttocks). As our goal was simply to identify many images for the elicitation we did not explore the reasons for exclusion in great detail.

5. Recruitment and incentives

As with the Mandarin Chinese - Guanzhong Dialect corpus, the present dataset was also collected by Juhong Zhan, Yue Jiang and their students from Xi'an Jiaotong University.

5.1 Recruitment

We recruited speakers of the Guanzhong dialect who had grown up in cities, counties, towns and countryside in the Guanzhong region, mainly Xi'an, Baoji, Xianyang, Weinan, Tongchuan and Yangling, etc., by posting recruitment notices on WeChat, a popular social media platform in China. For the sake of organization and management, we mainly targeted students from Xi'an Jiaotong University. The speakers needed to meet the following criteria

1. being born and growing up in Guanzhong region;
2. speaking Guanzhong dialect on a daily basis;
3. understanding English and being able to use a computer.

Participants were undergraduate students from Xi'an Jiaotong University and community members. They speak Guanzhong dialect with their families and town fellows, and Mandarin Chinese with teachers, classmates and friends who cannot understand and speak Guanzhong Dialect. They are able to freely switch between dialect and standard Mandarin.

The first task for the native Guanzhong dialect speakers was to record themselves naming the objects presented on a computer screen while speaking in their dialect (see Section 6). Each speaker was to identify and name each of 622 images using the Guanzhong dialect presented by the LanguageARC citizen science platform. We added the participants into a TenCent QQ group chat and sent them the project website and a video manual. All the speakers' questions and problems in the process of recording were answered online.

Once the recording was complete, the second task for the native speakers was quality control of the Guanzhong dialect (see §7). After automated and human effort at LDC to eliminate recordings containing digital artifacts, signal and noise problems, etc., native Guanzhong speakers were asked to judge whether the naming of the image was correct, whether the speaker was naming and not talking about the image, etc. In this second round, a total of 26 speakers participated, including some volunteer participants from the first round, and some newly recruited ones, to identify invalid recordings from those finished in the first, recording round. A tutorial video was posted with instructions on how to tag invalid recordings and the criteria for invalid recordings.

We recruited 48 participants for the recording task, 21 of whom participated in the quality control task. 18 male speakers and 30 females, mostly aged between 18-24, with only 3 over 30 participated in the recording task. Of those, 7 males and 14 females, mostly between the ages of 19-23, with one over 30 participated in the quality control task.

5.2 Incentives

A local language documentation task naturally presents several potential incentives to participants who may be attracted by their intellectual interest in language generally or in the specific dialect or by local pride and the opportunity to contribute to language preservation or by the task itself or the opportunity to work with others of like mind. Because the project was under time pressure to prepare a resource for possible use in a joint research project, we opted to augment these natural incentives of citizen science efforts.

Participants in the first task were awarded 100 yuan each, and since the recruited members were mostly students, two extra points were given to their daily performance as a reward for participation. In the quality control task, each participant tagging 1500 HITs received a standard reward of 300 yuan, with more pay for more work.

At the end of the assignment, we thanked the participants and paid them for their efforts one by one through online payment.

6. Collection

During collection we presented images to participants, one at a time, in random order and asked them to record themselves naming the items using the LanguageARC task picture in Figure 3. Participants could listen to their recording before submitting and make a new recording if they felt it necessary. Each naming took a few seconds to accomplish. Contributors could proceed at their own pace, skip items, leave the task and return as they wished. The task included a tutorial in standard Chinese on making high quality audio recordings. The speech collection ran from February through May 2021. As this effort was framed as a citizen science project in which maximizing participation is a goal, we did not require participants to use any specific computer hardware, browser or microphone.

Figure 3: Recording Object Namings

Throughout the collection (and QC) phases researchers at Xi'an Jiaotong University worked closely with LDC to discuss any problems that might arise. Based on our experience in the pilot task and reviews of early recordings, we identified and constantly reminded the participants of these important issues:

1. speaking too close to the microphone and/or too lead can lead to clipping;
2. low signal can result from the speaker being too far from the microphone, turning away from the microphone or speaking too softly;
3. environmental noise could reduce the value of the recordings;
4. the frequency of digital artifacts was significantly higher for some participants or environments; some were ask to try a different local or device;
5. forgetting to click "Submit" after recording could result in long recordings with little useable data;
6. clicking "Skip" too frequently cold skew the distribution of the data; participants who did so were encouraged to consult the team leader;
7. recordings could be reviewed and new recordings made as needed; participants were reminded to do this if they were uncertain about their naming or the system performance.

7. Quality Control

Initial review of the audio collected via LanguageARC, from test subjects in the US and China, revealed that quality was generally quite good with high SNR. However, as the number and diversity of speakers, systems, locations and clips grew, notwithstanding the care taken during collection, quality naturally varied according to participants' hardware and network capability, physical environments and behaviors.

Although LanguageARC relied upon an open source audio collection framework intended for use over the Internet, we experienced two types of problems: long sequences of samples with a value of 0 (nulls), presumably due to aggressive noise suppression, and stark discontinuities in the waveform, presumably due to packet loss, replication or interpolation. Although we have since adjusted the framework's parameters within LanguageARC to mitigate these problems, there were nonetheless audio samples that needed to be set aside.

At the scale the project worked, it seemed improbable that we could quality control all clips with human effort. Subsequently, we also learned that some recording problems were difficult to detect just by listening. For example, one of the commonest error patterns was a string of 127 null samples which, at the sampling rate used by the recording framework was just 2 milliseconds of silence and was often missed by human listeners. In addition, because collection had gone much better than expected (more speakers naming more objects) we could afford to set aside audio clips that revealed any undesirable properties and still have a suitable corpus. With this in mind we created a cascade of automatic and human QC processes that was intended to identify and set aside all recordings with digital artifacts and present the remainder for more careful review.

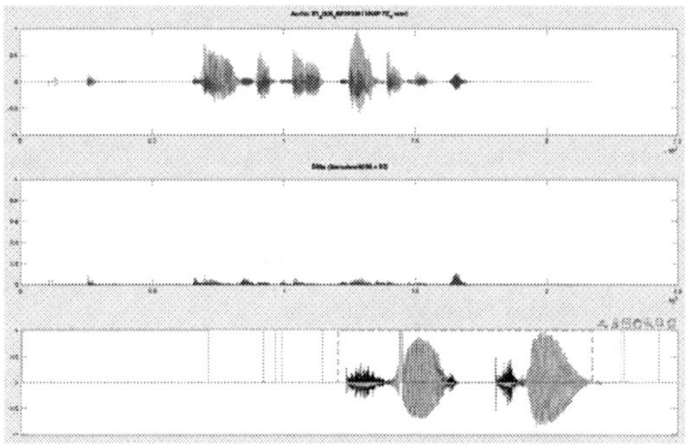

Figure 4: Automated Detection of Digitization Artefacts

7.1 Automated

To assure rapid QC of the very large number of clips collected we developed customized automated detectors in MatLab to identify any cases in which the audio contained sequences of zero-valued samples or large discontinuities in adjacent sample values during speech segments. These automatic detectors were correlated with human judgments of the same types of problems and adjusted until the automated methods were at least as sensitive as human ears. At that point, the automated detectors were used to preprocess the entire corpus. Any audio clip that suffered from either problem type was set aside and the remaining clips were subjected to further human QC. Figure 4 shows an interface used in developing the automated detectors. The panels, from top to bottom, contain: the waveform; a plot of the difference between adjacent sample values where large discontinuities appear as spikes (none apparent in this example); and a zoomed in display of a waveform showing a speech region (green box) and null sequences (orange and red boxes, the latter indicating null strings during speech).

7.2 Human Quality Control

In the second round, the criteria for invalid recordings were set as follows: recordings being incomplete or distorted; speech being too low and soft; noise being too loud; recordings in a dialect other than Guanzhong; or a naming mismatch to the image presented.

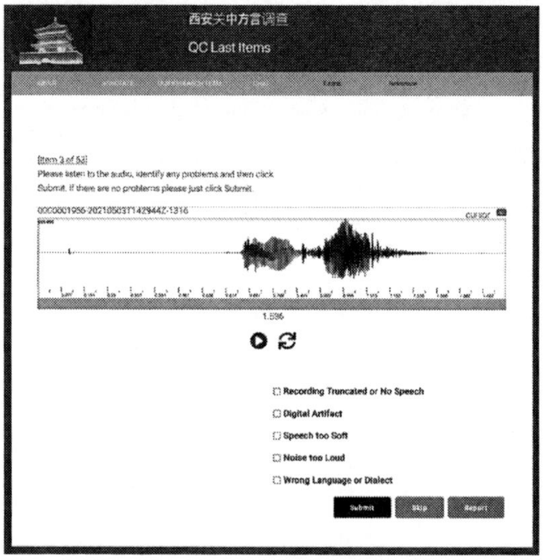

Figure 5: Human Quality Control of Audio Recordings

8. Resulting Data

The object naming task yielded 34,729 audio recordings in total. After automated quality control excluded clips for sequences of nulls or large discontinuities in the wave form and human quality control excluded clips that were truncated or still sounded as if they were marred by digital artifacts, 25,972 remained. Any of these annotated for the other problems: speech too soft, background noise too loud or contained lexical items in the wrong language/dialect were retained but appropriated marked in the metadata tables.

The corpus is organized into 622 directories according to the image presented. Each directory contains on average 42 recordings of namings of the object in the image (min=7, max=54, std=4.6) sampled at 16kHz, 16bit, single channel, WAV files. Files are named to indicate the image presented, a userID and the date and time of the recording. An accompanying table indicates, for each file, whether any human annotator indicated high noise, low signal or that the items is not in the target dialect. The table also provides the file size, duration of the audio file, duration of the speech portion and pseudo-SNR.

The corpus was originally released by LDC in September 2021 to participants in the Frontiers in AI Research Topic in *AI and Low-resource Speech Sciences* and will shortly be released to the entire research community.

9. Acknowledgements

The authors would like to express their gratitude to the US National Science Foundation (including CRI grant 1730377 which supports the NIEUW project described above); the Netherlands Organization for Scientific Research (NWO-VI.C.181.040) that funded related research on picture naming and data collection in under-studied languages; the University of Pennsylvania Office of the Vice Provost for Global Initiatives (PennGlobal) through its Penn China Research and Engagement Fund, and the University of Pennsylvania School of Arts and Sciences through its Global Engagement Fund that supported the creation of the Documenting Xi'an Guanzhong - Object Naming corpus and the Mandarin Chinese - Guanzhong Dialect corpus.

10. Bibliographical References

Bai, D. (1954). A Report on Guanzhong Dialect, Beijing, Chinese Academy of Sciences Press (in Chinese).

Chanchaochai, N., Cieri, C., Debrah, J., Ding, H., Jiang, Y., Liao, S., Liberman, M., Wright, J., Yuan, J., Zhan, J., Zhan, Y. (2018) GlobalTIMIT: Acoustic-Phonetic Datasets for the World's Languages, Proceedings of Interspeech.

Cieri, C., Fiumara, J. (2020) LanguageARC – a tutorial

LREC 2020: 12th Edition of the Language Resources and Evaluation Conference, CLLRD Workshop: Citizen Linguistics in Language Resource Development

Cieri, C., Fiumara, J., and Wright, J. (2021). Using Games to Augment Corpora for Language Recognition and Confusability, *Proc. 22nd Annual Conference of the International Speech Communication Association (Interspeech)*, August 30-September 3.

Duñabeitia, J.A, Crepaldi, D., Meyer, A. S., New, B., Pliatsikas, C., Smolka, E., and Brysbaert, M. (2018). MultiPic: A standardized set of 750 drawings with norms for six European languages. *Quarterly Journal of Experimental Psychology*. 71(4):808-816.

Fiumara, J., Cieri, C., Wright, J., and Liberman, M. (2020). LanguageARC: Developing Language Resources Through Citizen Linguistics in *Proc. 12th Edition of the Language Resources and Evaluation Conference (LREC)*. CLLRD Workshop: Citizen Linguistics in Language Resource Development. Marseille, May 11-16.

Joglekar, A, Seyed, O. S., Chandra-Shekar, M., Cieri, C., and Hansen, J.H.L. (2021). Fearless Steps Challenge Phase-3 (FSC P3): Advancing SLT for Unseen Channel and Mission Data Across NASA Apollo Audio in *Proc. 22nd Annual Conference of the International Speech Communication Association (Interspeech)*, August 30-September 3.

Li, R. (1989) Language Atlas of China, Longman.

Li Min. (2014). Study on Major Differences between Typical words in Guanzhong Dialect and Mandarin. Literature Education (01), 124-125.

Liu, M., Chen, Y., Schiller, N. O. (2020). Tonal mapping of Xi'an Mandarin and Standard Chinese. The Journal of the Acoustical Society of America, 147(4), 2803. https://doi.org/10.1121/10.0000993.

Lu Tuanhua. (2010). Comparison of the Phonetic Characteristics between Guanzhong Dialect and Mandarin. KAOSHI ZHOUKAN (09), 23-24.

Scholten, S., Merkx, D., Scharenborg, O., (2021) Learning to Recognise Words using Visually Grounded Speech, IEEE International Symposium on Circuits and Systems (ISCAS).

Sun Lixin. (2021). Complementary Discussions on Personal Pronouns in Guanzhong Dialect. Journal of Gansu Normal Colleges (01), 1-5.

Tardif, T. and Fletcher, P. Chinese Communicative Development Inventories: User's Guide and Manual (2008), Peking University Medical Press, Beijing, China.

Wang Wenya. (2015). Study on Phonetic and Lexical Features and History of Guanzhong dialect in Shaanxi Province. China Juveniles (22), 169-170.

Wang Yuding. (1995). Studies On Types of Sound Changes in the Guanzhong Dialect. Journal of Yan'an University (Social Sciences Edition).

Xing Xiangdong. (2014). The Key Investigations and Researches on Dialects in Northwest Regions—Mainly on Gansu, Ningxia, Qinghai, and Xinjiang Provinces. Journal of Tsinghua University (Philosophy and Social Sciences) (05), 122-134+178. Doi: 10.13613/j.cnki.qhdz.002267.

Zhang, W. J. (2005). Drifting and Competition: The Changes of the phonological structure of Guanzhong dialect. Shaanxi People's Publishing House.

Zhao Nana. (2020). A Research Review on Guanzhong Dialect Vocabulary. Journal of Jilin TV & Radio University (04),140-142.

Zhao Yonggang. (2017). Chinese Tone Sandhi and the Regional Differences of Citation Tones of Shaanxi Dialect. Foreign Language and Literature Research. 3(4), 12.

11. Language Resource References

Cieri, C., Zhan, J., Jiang, Y., Liberman, M., Yuan, J., Chen, Y., Scharenborg, O. (2021) Documenting Xi'an Guanzhong - Object Naming LDC2021E14. Web Download. Philadelphia: Linguistic Data Consortium,.

Garofolo, J., Lamel, L. Fisher, W., Fiscus, J., Pallett, D., Dahlgren, N., Zue, V. (1993) TIMIT Acoustic-Phonetic Continuous Speech Corpus LDC93S1. Web Download. Philadelphia: Linguistic Data Consortium.

Jiang, Y., Zhan, J., Han, H., Xu, Z., Zhou, H., Yuan, J., Liberman, M. (2020) Global TIMIT Mandarin Chinese-Guanzhong Dialect LDC2020S12. Web Download. Philadelphia: Linguistic Data Consortium.

Crowdsourced Participants' Accuracy at Identifying the Social Class of Speakers from South East England

Amanda Cole
Department of Language and Linguistics, University of Essex, Wivenhoe Park, Colchester, Essex, UK
amanda.cole@essex.ac.uk

Abstract

Five participants, each located in distinct locations (USA, Canada, South Africa, Scotland and (South East) England), identified the self-determined social class of a corpus of 227 speakers (born 1986–2001; from South East England) based on 10-second passage readings. This pilot study demonstrates the potential for using crowdsourcing to collect sociolinguistic data, specifically using LanguageARC, especially when geographic spread of participants is desirable but not easily possible using traditional fieldwork methods. Results show that, firstly, accuracy at identifying social class is relatively low when compared to other factors, including when the same speech stimuli were used (e.g., ethnicity: Cole 2020). Secondly, participants identified speakers' social class significantly better than chance for a three-class distinction (working, middle, upper) but not for a six-class distinction. Thirdly, despite some differences in performance, the participant located in South East England did not perform significantly better than other participants, suggesting that the participant's presumed greater familiarity with sociolinguistic variation in the region may not have been advantageous. Finally, there is a distinction to be made between participants' ability to pinpoint a speaker's exact social class membership and their ability to identify the speaker's relative class position. This paper discusses the role of social identification tasks in illuminating how speech is categorised and interpreted.

Keywords: social class; social identification tasks; language variation and change; sociolinguistics; citizen linguistics, crowdsourcing; South East England

1. Introduction

The extent to which people can identify another person's class from their speech is an important consideration in sociolinguistics for two principal reasons. Firstly, social identification tasks - in which participants attempt to identify social information about a person such as class, ethnicity, gender, age or sexuality from speech stimuli - inform us of how different social categories are referenced in participants' minds from speech. Patterns of accuracy in social identification tasks reveal to what extent different social labels and groupings are meaningful categories for participants and to what extent participants have accurate linguistic representations of these social groupings (see Campbell-Kibler 2010 for an overview). Secondly, social identification tasks aid our understanding of how discrimination and stereotyping are linked to linguistic variation. If social information about a person can be identified from speech, then this contributes to our understanding of linguistic profiling and the ways evaluations or judgements are made about people based on their speech. This paper presents the results of a pilot study, exploring participants' accuracy at identify the social class of speakers from South East England.

1.1 Social Identification Tasks

Accuracy at social identification tasks is in part related to the link between a social group and linguistic features. In sociolinguistics, the term "indexicality" refers to the ideological relationship between linguistic features and a social group, persona, characteristic or place that they signal (see Silverstein 2003; Eckert 2008). Linguistic features can be indexing of so-called macro-social groups such as class, gender, ethnicity or micro-categories which reflect local identities (e.g. "jocks" vs "burnouts" in Detroit: Eckert, 1989).

There are different orders of indexicalities (see Silverstein 2003). There could simply be correlations between social factors and linguistic features which do not attract overt commentary. At the opposite extreme, features may be socially salient such that people may perform, discuss, interpret and evaluate them. These linguistic features may become enregistered such that, following Johnstone's definition of enregisterment (2009: 159), linguistic features are linked with specific labels. In the same way that people may associate certain speech patterns with labels such as "Pittsburghese" (Johnstone, 2009), "Geordie" (Beal, 2018) or "chav" (Cole & Tieken, 2021), people may hold concepts of the way that different social class groupings such as "lower-working class" speak which may or may not be an accurate representation. In this way, social identification tasks shed some important insights into the links that participants make between speech and social groupings.

In addition, social identification tasks are important as they aid our understanding of how discrimination and stereotyping may be facilitated through linguistic perception and profiling. Purnell et al. (1999) demonstrated that in the US, a person's ethnicity could be determined from as little as the word *hello.* If social information about a person such as their ethnicity can be determined from their speech, then so too, speech can act as a vehicle for profiling and stereotyping. The authors also showed that when the same person inquired about a flat to let in a Standard American accent, they were more likely to receive a positive outcome such as an invitation to view the apartment than if they spoke in an African American or Chicano American accent (Purnell et al. 1999). If identifications about a person's social or demographic background can be made from speech alone, then the evaluations or judgements made about a person based on their speech can be a window into broader societal prejudice.

Previous work has shown that the lower a person's class in South East England, the more harshly they are judged, for instance on measures such as intelligence and friendliness (Cole 2021). In addition, it has been shown that when participants are instructed to assess potential candidates' interview performance and perceived hirability for a trainee

Proceedings of the 2nd Workshop on Novel Incentives in Data Collection from People @LREC2022, pages 38–45
Marseille, 25 June 2022.

solicitor position at a corporate law firm, there is a particular bias against "candidates" who spoke working-class varieties from the South of England (Levon et al. 2021). Though studies have shown that working-class speakers are disadvantaged by their accent (which in itself is a marker that they are working class), there has not been substantive research into how accurately people's social class can be identified from their speech. This knowledge is an important component to understanding a fuller picture of how speech is perceived, categorised but also judged and evaluated in relation to social class.

1.2 Linguistic Variation and Class in Britain

Social class (or "class"), along with age, gender and ethnicity, is one of the most frequently studied social factors in sociolinguistics. The recurrent finding in a plethora of sociolinguistic production work in Britain, as well as many other locations, is that the lower a person's class, the more likely they are to use vernacular features. In contrast, the higher a person's class, the more likely they are to use standard features (see Cole, forthcoming for an overview).

Trudgill (2001) envisages linguistic variation in Britain as a triangle shape with social class on the y-axis and regional variation on the x-axis at the base of the triangle. In essence, the lower a person's social class, represented at the base of the triangle, the greater linguistic variation. This means that working-class people tend to speak in ways that are regionally marked and vary, often substantially, to the dialects of other working-class people from different places to them. In contrast, as social class increases, the less regional variation is found. At the extreme, at the tip of the triangle, the highest classes in Britain are presumed to speak almost identically to each other, converging on Received Pronunciation (RP) (often called "Queen's English"). RP is an accent exemplified by the higher classes that is spoken across the country and is often defined as not being regionally marked, i.e., is not linked to where a person is from (Trudgill, 2001). It is well established then that the lower a person's class the more regional productions in their speech. It seems, then, like a sound, though to my knowledge an untested, hypothesis that the reverse is also true: the more regional productions in a person's speech, the lower their class. Following this, if participants are attuned to the structure of sociolinguistic variation in Britain, they may be able to infer a person's class by the degree of regional pronunciations in their speech.

It is worth emphasising that sociolinguistic variation is a matter of probabilities. A working-class person is more likely to have a regional pronunciation at a higher rate than a middle-class person. It is very rarely the case that middle-class people will never produce a feature and it is produced without exception in the speech of working-class people from the same speech community. It is much more probable that the feature will be produced by both working-class and middle-class speakers but at different rates. Therefore, sociolinguistic variation is, at least in terms of social class, group-preferential and not group-exclusive. Following this, in a social class identification task, it is not simply the case that if a participant hears a regional linguistic feature they can be assured that the speaker is working-class. These features will also most likely be used by some middle-class speakers in the same community, but presumably to a lesser extent. Social class identification tasks test to what extent participants are attuned to sociolinguistic variation and can base probabilistic assumptions about a person's class from speech stimuli.

1.3 Accuracy at Social Class Identification Tasks

Previous research on social class identifications from speech has been very limited. There have been previous studies on how linguistic variation is perceived in relation to social class. For instance, in New Zealand, Hay et al. (2006) asked participants to listen to audio stimuli which could be variably interpreted as two different words due to a vowel merger in the speech community. If participants were led to believe that they are hearing a working-class speaker, they are more likely to believe they heard productions that are more common in working-class speakers. Buchstaller (2006) played matched-guise (produced by a single speaker) audio clips with variable rates of quotative *go* to see if this would effect to what extent British participants perceived the speaker as working class.

However, there have not been, to my knowledge, comprehensive studies testing to what extent speakers' social class can be identified from speech stimuli. Though social class has been neglected in social identification tasks, previous research has explored participants' accuracy at identifying various other social factors from speech stimuli: ethnicity/race (Purnell et al., 1999; Holliday & Jaggers, 2015; Cole 2020), age (O'Cain, 2000), sexuality and perceived masculinity/femininity (Munson 2007; Levon, 2014) and location (McKenzie, 2015). These studies have shown that firstly, not all speaker groups are identified with equal accuracy, which is often related to the saliency of the different categories and their associated linguistic features. Secondly, not all participant groups perform the task with equal accuracy which is often conditioned by participants' familiarity or exposure to relevant linguistic variation (see Clopper & Pisoni, 2004).

As a result, though no predictions are made about the direction of the effect in this present study, it may be that some social classes are identified more accurately than others and/or that it is easier to identify the social class of either men or women. In addition, the primary hypothesis of this paper is that the participant located in South East England will perform the task with highest accuracy. There are five participants in the study, each located in a different place: USA, Canada, South Africa, Scotland and (South East) England. In much the same way that a geographic proximity effect is found in participants' ability to identify speakers' geographic provenance (Montgomery, 2012), this paper predicts that the participant located in South East England will perform with highest accuracy. It is probable that they are most familiar with patterns of sociolinguistic variation and the class structure in South East England.

2. Methods

This study uses crowdsourcing through LanguageARC to collect data on levels of accuracy in the identification of speakers' social class from speech stimuli. This paper is based on data collected through a LanguageARC project (see Cieri et al., 2018; 2019), *From Cockney to the Queen*, which examines how language in South East England is produced, categorised and evaluated in relation to place, class and ethnicity (see Cole 2020 for further findings from this project). LanguageArc is an online resource which allows researchers to create language resources which members of the public can participate in (Cieri et al., 2018, 2019). LanguageARC encourages members of the public, or "Citizen Linguists", to spare as little or as much time as they would like to contribute to linguistic research. The *From Cockney to the Queen* project was open for a limited period of time and participants for this study were not overtly recruited, but instead, participated in the task as part of their contribution more generally to LanguageARC.

2.1 Research Questions

Can participants accurately identify the class of speakers significantly better than chance and is their accuracy affected by:

a) speakers' gender?
b) speakers' social class?
c) participants' location (South East England; Scotland; USA; South Africa; Canada)?

2.2 Participants

In this study, the results of five participants are presented, each located in a different English-speaking area: (South East) England, Scotland, USA, South Africa and Canada. LanguageARC indicates the location of the participant at the point they took part in the experiment. It is not known how long participants have spent in that location or their linguistic background or levels of exposure to south-eastern varieties of English. More information such as age, gender and social class is not known about the participants.

It is also acknowledged that there is a very small number of participants in this present study due in part to the limited period of time that the project was open for contributions. The results presented are a pilot study and are tentative. This paper presents a case study, demonstrating how sociolinguistic data can be collected for sociolinguistic studies through crowdsourcing, specifically using LanguageARC. An advantage of this approach is that participants were not recruited to the task and instead, they completed it for their own enjoyment or desire to contribute to research. It is therefore likely that, though there was a very limited number of participants, they have engaged closely with the task.

In addition, through LanguageArc, participants from all over the world can easily contribute to research as long as they have an internet connection and willingness. This overcomes some confounding factors that sociolinguists may face when recruiting participants, for instance, people from different locations or with different linguistic backgrounds who are recruited through their similar experience living or studying in a single location. Although crowdsourcing is often considered for large-scale collection, it can also benefit collections where geographic spread is desirable but not possible using traditional fieldwork methods. The comparison of the person located in South East England and other locations around the world would have been difficult without the crowdsourcing platform.

2.3 Stimuli and Procedure

Participants heard speech stimuli taken from a corpus of 227 speakers from South East England. The order of the speech stimuli was randomised for each individual participant. For each speaker, participants heard an approximately 10-second audio clip extracted from a passage reading. Participants then selected the class of the speaker from six options: "lower working", "upper working", "lower middle", "upper middle", "lower upper" and "upper upper" or they had the choice to skip that speaker. A two-tier system was used within each class (e.g., working class was split into lower- and upper-working). This decision was made in order to align findings with production studies where this same division of classes is made. For instance, it has previously been acknowledged that the lower-middle class and upper-working class are key in leading language change (have highest rates of incoming variants for a variable in a process of change) (e.g., Labov 2001; see Cole, forthcoming for discussion on class divisions in sociolinguistics).

"Lower upper" and "upper upper" were included as possible selections even though it may seem improbable that participants come into regular contact with upper class speakers in day-to-day life. However, this study did not want to make any prior assumptions about participants' backgrounds or their conceptions of the class structure or what constitutes each class. The "lower upper" and "upper upper" values were included to give participants the full range of options without making prior assumptions. In addition, "upper class" was also split into "lower" and "upper" so as to mirror the values added for both working- and middle-class. It is possible that including such a broad range may have affected the judgements of participants as they may have felt they needed to use the full range of responses. Nonetheless, if participants do indeed hold associations for the specific class labels then the full range of responses would not greatly skew participants' accuracy. In addition, participants' accuracy was tested not only as a binary outcome (correct classification vs. incorrect classification) but also as a correlation between speakers' class and participants' responses.

The audio clips were lexically identical and were taken from passage readings which were recorded as part of a larger study on language production and perception in South East England (see Cole, 2021). Although spontaneous speech would likely lead to a higher rate of vernacular features, a reading passage was chosen to control for contextual information or lexical choice. Each clip lasted approximately 10 seconds and was taken from a reading of the same sentence which was chosen to include a range of linguistic variables known to be variable or important in South East England such as (T)-glottalling, (ING), (H)-dropping, (L)-vocalisation and variation in the vowel system. This paper does not have the scope but future research could investigate which linguistic variables and variants lead speakers to be identified as a certain class. The sentence selected was:

"The sky is falling", cried Chicken Little. His head hurt and he could feel a big painful bump on it. "I'd better warn the others", and off he raced in a panicked cloud of fluff.

All speakers were aged between 18 and 33 ($\overline{x} = 21.8$; SD = 3.2). They had all lived in South East England for at least half of the years between the ages of 3 and 18. The speakers came from a wide range of locations across South East England which was defined generously. There was at least one speaker from each borough of London as well as the following counties: Cambridgeshire, Oxfordshire, Essex, Hertfordshire, Berkshire, Buckinghamshire, East Sussex, West Sussex, Hampshire, Suffolk, Surrey, Kent and Bedfordshire.

Of the speakers, 41 identified as lower-working class, 54 as upper working, 81 as lower middle, 47 as upper middle, three as lower upper and one as upper upper. Speakers identified their own social class. They selected their social class from the six pre-mentioned choices. Often, sociolinguists impose social class classifications on speakers, most often based on a metric of socio-economic indicators. Nonetheless, as it has not been evidenced to what extent this translates to self-defined groupings, in this study, speakers identified their own class. In this way, class was meaningful to the speakers and not outwardly defined, but it is also not clear what extent their social class identity translates to conventional measures of social class position.

2.4 Analysis

A consideration with LanguageARC is that each participant could complete as many or as few of the 277 judgements as they wished. The task did not have to be completed in one sitting, and participants could return to the task at any point and pick up where they left off. In fact, Citizen Linguists at LanguageARC are encouraged to dip into tasks even if they only wish to spare a few minutes. Though this approach encourages active engagement, it also means that there will almost always be an imbalance in the datapoints collected for each participant. Also, as participants do not have to complete the task in full, not all speakers are heard by all participants.

There was a total of 146 datapoints, excluding the 19 instances participants skipped a speaker rather than attempt to identify a speaker's class. In addition, upper-class speakers, of whom there was only four, were only heard a combined total of three times. As a result, identifications made of the four upper-class speakers were not included in the analysis.
In spite of this, participants could identify speakers' class from the 6-way distinction (i.e. including "lower-upper" and "upper-upper" class. This means that, in this analysis, on any instance that a participant considered a speaker to be either lower- or upper-upper class, they were not correct. However, it is still of interest to know which speakers, if any, were considered to be upper class as this provides insights into participants' perceptual representation of the class system.

Of the 227 speakers in the corpus of speech stimuli, at least one identification was made for 115 speakers. Of the 146 judgements, 28 were made of lower-working speakers, 38 of upper working, 55 of lower middle, and 25 of upper middle. This pattern roughly matched the distribution of speakers' social classes. For instance, as mentioned, more speakers identified as lower-middle class than any other class and correspondingly, more lower-middle class speakers were heard by participants than any other class. In addition, there was an imbalance in the contribution of each participant. Of the 146 judgements, 67, 19, 20, 32 and 8 identifications were made by the participants located in South East England, South Africa, Scotland, Canada and the USA respectively.

The analysis was split into three parts. Firstly, it was tested whether participants' accuracy at identifying speakers' social class was better than chance. A one-sample Wilcoxon test was selected due to the non-parametric distribution of the datapoints. This test compared participants' average accuracy against the 1/6 probability of choosing the correct category out of chance.

Secondly, a logistic regression was run in R using the glm function to test whether the gender or social class of speakers or the location of participants predicted the accuracy of the class identifications. The dependent variable in the model was the participants' accuracy for each judgement: a two-level categorical variable coded as either "yes" or "no". Lower-working class was the reference level for the class variable as the extreme of the scale. South East England was the reference level for the participant location variable as the obvious baseline of comparison and due to the hypothesis that this participant would perform with highest rates of accuracy. For all comparisons, α was set at 0.05.

Thirdly, a Kendall's correlation was run to test the ordinal association between the two ranked variables for each participant: speakers' actual social class and the social class the participant classified them as. If a participant considers a lower-working class speaker as upper-working class, this seems is a more accurate judgement than considering the same speaker to be upper-middle class. The Kendall's correlation test established if there were positive correlations in participants' performance. That is, did they tend to consider lower-class speakers as of a lower class than they tended to consider higher-class speakers to be?

3. Results

3.1 Did Participants Perform Better than Chance?

Participants made relatively balanced selections between the six choices: there were 18, 27, 29, 43, 17 and 12 selections for "lower working", "upper working", "lower middle", "upper middle", "lower upper" and "upper upper" respectively. Participants were more likely to consider speakers to be middle class, particularly upper-middle class, compared to any other class group.

Participants had relatively low rates of accuracy when identifying the class of speakers, with an average across all judgements and all participants of 21.9% (32/146). As a point of comparison, based on the same speech stimuli and LanguageARC project, previous research (Cole 2020) explored participants' accuracy at identifying the ethnicity of speakers into the main "ethnic" groups in Britain according to the UK Census: White British, Black British and Asian British. In this study, participants found perceptual linguistic differences between speakers of all 3 ethnicities, averaging 80.7% accuracy at the task. The highest rate of accuracy (96%) was when identifying the ethnicity of Black British speakers from London whose speech seems to form a distinct, perceptual category. It is not the case then that there is no or very limited linguistic variation present in the speech stimuli, instead, participants in this present study could not identify class with the same accuracy that ethnicity was previously identified from the same speech stimuli.

On the whole, a one-sample Wilcoxon test did not find participants' rates of accuracy to be significantly greater than chance. It seems that participants do not have a 6-way class distinction, or at least, not one that translates to accuracy at linguistic identifications. However, when responses were amassed into three classes (working, middle and upper), a one-sample Wilcoxon test found that accuracy rates were significantly greater than chance averaging 47.3% (69/146) (p=0.03) (see Figure 1).

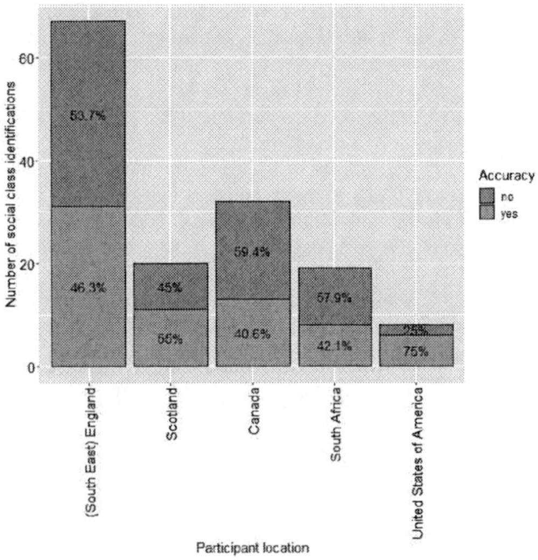

Figure 1: Participant location (one participant per location) and their accuracy at identifying speakers' social class from speech stimuli. Participants' average performance was significantly greater than chance when identifying class from a 3-way distinction (working, middle, upper). Compared to the baseline of South-East England, there were no significant differences in participants' rates of accuracy.

3.2 Which Factors Predict Participants' Accuracy?

There were no significant effects in the logistic regression model. There was a trend that women's class was identified more accurately than that of men (26.3% and 17.1% accuracy for female and male speakers respectively) but the effect was not significant (p=0.057) (Figure 2). In addition, accuracy was not greater when identifying any specific social class. The rates of accuracy for identifying speakers from each class were 21.4%, 21%, 20% and 28% for lower-working, upper-working, lower-middle and upper-middle class speakers respectively (Figure 3).

There were no significant differences in accuracy rates between participants. Participants performed with similar rates of accuracy when identifying the class of speakers (see Figure 1). This is with the exception of the participant in the USA who performed with higher rates of accuracy than other but this difference was not significant and this participant had many less datapoints than the other participants. Though it was hypothesised that the participant located in South East England would perform significantly better than other participants, this was not found to be the case. The lack of significant effects in the model for the gender and class of speakers as well as the location of participants was also found to be true when the test was re-run with a three-class distinction.

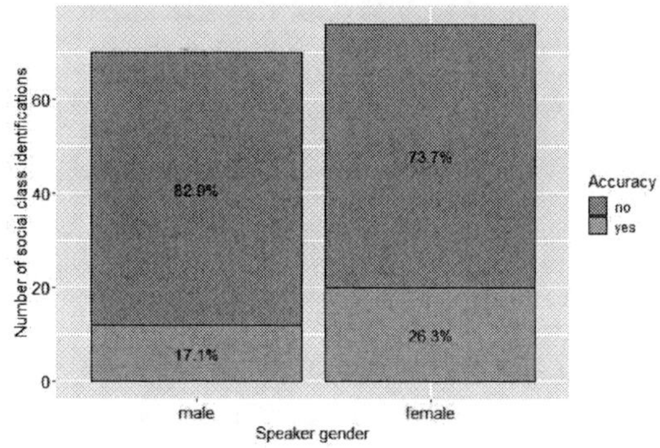

Figure 2: Speakers' gender and the accuracy with which their social class was identified from speech stimuli. Though women's social class was accurately identified more often than men's, the effect was not significant (p=0.057).

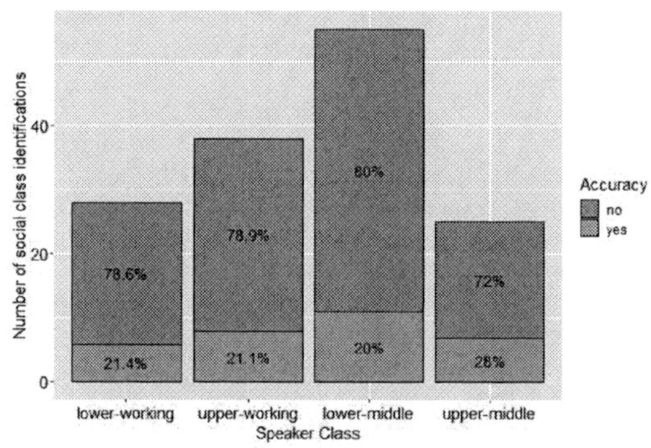

Figure 3: Speakers' social class and how accurately their class was identified from speech stimuli. There were no significant effects.

3.3 Is there Correlation between Speakers' Class and how they are Classified?

A Kendall's correlation test explored the relationship between speakers' social class and the classifications made by the participants. A significant correlation was only found for the South East participant and no others. For this participant there was a weak, yet significant correlation (p = 0.021; Tau = 0.23).

For instance, as shown in Figure 4, this participant accurately classified lower-middle class speakers as lower-middle class on six instances and inaccurately as upper-middle class on 10 instances. They very infrequently considered the participant to be working class (one and two instances for lower and upper respectively) or upper class (four and two instances for lower and upper respectively). In contrast, a lower-working class speaker was only correctly identified as lower-working class on two instances, but most frequently (on five instances) they were thought to be upper working class. These results further indicate that the participant's linguistic representation of the class system is more closely aligned with a three-way class system than a six-way system.

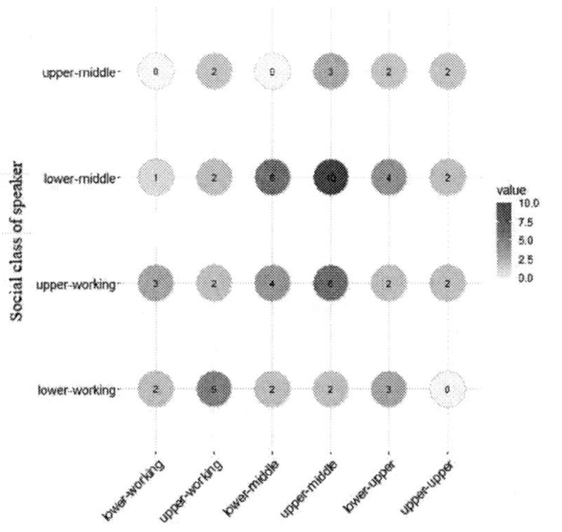

Figure 4: Results of a participant located in South East England when identifying the social class of speakers from this region. The social class selected by the participant and social class of speakers are weakly but significantly correlated (p-value = 0.021; Tau = 0.23).

This trend mostly held with the exception of upper-working class speakers. The class of these speakers was accurately identified on only two instances and they were considered lower-working class on three instances. They were most often considered to be middle class (four and six instances for lower-middle and upper-middle class respectively). It may be that upper-working class speakers do not speak in a way that allows them to be accurately identified as working class. Instead, they speak in a way more similar to participants' perceptual representation of middle-class speech. This is reminiscent of Labov's (see 1966, 1972) previous assertations that lower-middle and upper-working class speakers have the most social and linguistic 'insecurity' and consequentially, they use standard features to a greater extent than would be expected relative to their bordering classes, reflecting their aspirations of upward social mobility. Further research could look at exploring this in more detail with greater participant numbers.

4. Discussion

Participants' accuracy was significantly better than chance when identifying speakers' class in a three-way distinction (working, middle, upper) but not for a six-way distinction (lower working, upper working, lower middle, upper middle, lower upper, upper upper). When exploring the effect of social factors on patterns of linguistic variation and change, sociolinguists typically divide up social class with a two-way distinction within each class (e.g., working class is split into upper- and lower- working etc.). Though sociolinguists have often found variation within this fine-grained class system, it does not seem that participants were attuned to this variation as they did not make accurate class identifications in the six-way class division. Given that sociolinguists' class system apparently does not resonate with contributors, it may be that in future research, alternative comparisons could provide interesting insights into how class is perceived and categorised from linguistic stimuli. For example, participants could judge the relative class position of speakers e.g., whether they are the same class or if one speaker is of a higher or lower class than the other(s).

Rates of accuracy at the task were not significantly affected by either speakers' gender or social class. In addition, there were no significant differences in rates of accuracy between the five participants. In contrast to the paper's prediction, the participant located in South East England did not perform significantly better than the other participants. Though it was predicted that this participant would have greater familiarity with sociolinguistic variation and social class structures in South East England, they did not perform significantly better than other participants. This finding is reminiscent of the results of the pre-mentioned study in which, based on the same speech stimuli as this present study, participants were asked to identify the ethnicity of speakers from South East England (Cole, 2020). The five participants located in Britain did not perform significantly better than the five participants in the US.

Both ethnicity and class are macro social categories, and perhaps a geographic proximity effect would be found for more locally-meaningful, micro categories. As discussed, the structure of sociolinguistic variation in Britain is strongly related to social class i.e., the higher the social class, the lesser the regional variation. Following this, in order to complete this task, participants only needed to be attuned to the general principle of sociolinguistic variation in Britain: the closer a speaker is to RP, the higher their class. Previous work has shown that people in the US are familiar with RP and the accent is associated with notions of prestige and correctness (Stewart et al., 1985). It was perhaps not necessary to be familiar with south-eastern varieties but instead, to be able to discern the degree of difference from RP for each speaker, which may explain the lack of significant differences in participants' performance.

Nonetheless, there was an important difference in the performance of the participant located in South East England compared to other participants. For this participant, and none other, there was a significant correlation between the speakers' class and the class that they were classified as by the participant. Therefore, to some extent, this participant did perform more accurately than others but this difference was not found when accuracy was considered as a binary outcome. The South East England participant was somewhat attuned to the general trend of the relative class position of the person whose speech they heard, but this did not clearly translate to a clear ability to pinpoint which specific class a speaker pertained to.

As discussed, the results of a social class identification task are of interest to sociolinguists for two main reasons. Firstly, if a person's social or demographic factors can be identified from speech, then this provides insights into the ways that profiling and discriminatory practices can take place based on a person's speech (see Purnell et al., 1999). Accuracy at the class identification task was relatively low and was only significantly greater than chance for a three-way class distinction. Nonetheless, this does not mean that, based on speech stimuli, people of different classes face equal evaluations. As discussed, there is much previous evidence that in southern England, based on their speech, speakers of working-class accents are disadvantaged (Cole, 2021; Levon et al., 2022).

Nonetheless, linguistic variation is perhaps not overtly linked to social class in the minds of listeners. When participants heard speech that was strongly regionally-marked, this may not have overtly and explicitly indexed the label "working class" and even less so "lower-working class". In fact, this is perhaps why prejudice and negative attitudes towards working-class speech patterns are so pervasive in British society; there is not a salient awareness that these ideas contribute towards and bolster societal inequalities related to a person's social class. Instead, speech that is heavily regionally-marked may be considered in other framings such as incorrect, not proper or lazy rather than a marker of a person's social class despite the objective linguistic reality of linguistic variation by class.

This links with the other previously mentioned reason why social identification tasks are of importance to sociolinguists. These tasks can go some way to revealing if social labels are meaningful categories for participants and to what extent participants have accurate linguistic representations of these social groupings. Participants did not seem generally attuned with the linguistic make-up of the class groupings used in this study. Participants performed with higher accuracy for the three-way class distinction than the six-way distinction, but accuracy was relatively low across the task. Generally, the labels were not accurately referenced in participants' minds by the combinations of linguistic features they heard produced by the speakers.

However, these findings do not rule out the possibility that participants do explicitly associate specific ways of speaking with these class labels. Firstly, this paper tested participants ability to identify a person's class identity and not their class per se. It may be that there is not a clear alignment between social class as determined by objective criteria and social class identity. It is possible that rates of accuracy at the class identification task would have been different if class was determined and defined differently. Secondly, it may be that the linguistic features which index social class labels were not present in the stimuli presented to participants. However, as mentioned there was sufficient linguistic variation in the speech stimuli that in a previous study based on the same speech stimuli (Cole 2020), participants could identify speakers' ethnicity with much greater accuracy (averaging 80.7%). Thirdly, it may be that participants do indeed associate the linguistic features present in the speech stimuli with specific class labels but that this did not translate to accuracy at the task. Buchstaller (2006) has previously shown that British participants overtly associate quotatative *go* with the working class. However, when played matched-guise audio clips with variable rates of *go*, the participants did not believe that participants with higher rates of *go* were more likely to be working class. It is not necessarily the case that what participants' overtly associate with a label is entirely equitable with how they actually perceive and categorise speech stimuli.

In sum, this paper has presented the results of a pilot study testing the extent to which participants can identify another person's social class from their speech and which factors condition accuracy. This study has shown the potential for collecting sociolinguistic data with crowdsourcing, specifically using LanguageARC. This is a pilot study with a small number of participants so results are necessarily tentative. However, some interesting results have emerged. Firstly, accuracy at identifying social class is relatively low, for instance when compared to other factors in comparable studies (e.g.,ethnicity: Cole 2020). Secondly, participants could not identify speakers' social class significantly better than chance from a six-class distinction but they could for a three-class distinction. Thirdly, though there were some different patterns of responses, the participant located in South East England did not perform with significantly greater accuracy than other participants, suggesting familiarity with sociolinguistic variation in the region may not have been very advantageous. Finally, there is a distinction to be made between participants ability to pinpoint a speaker's exact social class membership and their ability to identify their relative class position. This paper has discussed these results in the context of how social identification tasks can illuminate patterns in how speech is categorised and interpreted.

5. References

Beal, J. (2018). Dialect as heritage. In A. Creese, A. Blackledge (Eds), The Routledge Handbook of Language and Superdiversity. Abingdon, Oxon./New York: Routledge, pp. 165–180.

Buchstaller, I. (2006). Social stereotypes, personality traits and regional perception displaced: Attitudes towards the 'new'quotatives in the UK. Journal of Sociolinguistics, 10(3), pp. 362-381.

Campbell-Kibler, K. (2010). Sociolinguistics and perception. *Language and Linguistics Compass* 4(6), pp. 377-389.

Cieri, C., Fiumara, J., Liberman, M., Callison-Burch, C., and Wright, J. (2018). Introducing NIEUW: Novel Incentives and Workflows for Eliciting Linguistic Data *Proceedings of the 11th Edition of the Language Resources and Evaluation Conference (LREC 2018).* Pages 151-155, Miyazaki, May 7-12.

Cieri, C., Write, J., Fiumara, J., Shelmire, A. and Liberman, M. (2019). LanguageARC: Using Citizen Science to Augment Sociolinguistic Data Collection and Coding

NWAV48: New Ways of Analyzing Variation Eugene, October 10-12.
Clopper, C. G., and Pisoni, D. B. (2004). Homebodies and army brats: some effects of early linguistic experience and residential history on dialect categorization. *Language Variation and Change* 16(1), pp.31–48.
Cole, A. (forthcoming). Perceptions and Class. In: C. Montgomery, C., E. Moore. Oxford Handbook of British Englishes. Oxford University Press.
Cole, A. (2020). Identifications of Speaker Ethnicity in South-East England: Multicultural London English as a Divisible Perceptual Variety. In J. Fiumara, C. Cieri, M. Liberman, C. Callison-Burch, (Eds), Proceedings of the LREC 2020 Workshop on Citizen Linguistics in Language Resource Development, pp. 49-57
Cole, A. (2021). Disambiguating language attitudes held towards socio-demographic groups and geographic areas in South East England. Journal of Linguistic Geography 9 (1), pp. 13-27
Cole, A. & Tieken-Boon van Ostade, I. (2021). Haagse Harry, a Dutch chav from The Hague? The enregisterment of similar social personas in different speech communities. International Journal of Language and Culture.
Dailey-O'Cain, J. (2000). The sociolinguistic distribution of and attitudes toward focuser like and quotative like. Journal of Sociolinguistics 4(1), pp. 60-80.
Eckert, P. (1989). Jocks and burnouts: Social categories and identity in the high school. Teachers college press.
Eckert, P. (2008). Variation and the indexical field. Journal of sociolinguistics 12(4), pp. 453-476.
Hay, J., Warren, P. & Drager, K. (2006). Factors influencing speech perception in the context of a merger-in-progress. Journal of Phonetics 34(4), pp. 458-484.
Holliday, N.R. & Jaggers, Z. (2015). Influence of suprasegmental features on perceived ethnicity of American politicians. In Proceedings of ICPhS 2015.
Johnstone, B. (2009). Pittsburghese shirts: Commodification and the enregisterment of an urban dialect. American Speech 84(2), pp. 157–175.
Labov, W. (1966). *The social stratification of English in New York City*. Washington, DC: Centre for Applied Linguistics.
Labov, W. (1972). *Sociolinguistic Patterns*. Philadelphia: University of Pennsylvania Press.
Levon, E. (2014). Categories, stereotypes, and the linguistic perception of sexuality. Language in Society 43(5), pp. 539-566.
Levon, E., Sharma, D., Watt, D.J., Cardoso, A. & Ye, Y. (2021). Accent Bias and Perceptions of Professional Competence in England. Journal of English Linguistics 49(4), pp. 355-388.
McKenzie, R.M. (2015). The sociolinguistics of variety identification and categorisation: Free classification of varieties of spoken English amongst non-linguist listeners. Language Awareness 24(2), pp. 150-168.
Munson, B. (2007). The acoustic correlates of perceived masculinity, perceived femininity, and perceived sexual orientation. Language and Speech 50(1), pp.125-142.
Purnell, T., Idsardi, W., & Baugh, J. (1999). Perceptual and phonetic experiments on American English dialect identification. Journal of language and social psychology 18(1), pp. 10-30.
Silverstein, M. (2003). Indexical order and the dialectics of sociolinguistic life. Language & Communication 23(3-4), pp. 193-229
Stewart, M.A., Ryan, E.B. & Giles, H. (1985). Accent and social class effects on status and solidarity evaluations. Personality and social psychology bulletin 11(1), pp. 98-105.
Trudgill, P. (2001). Sociolinguistic Variation and Change. Edinburgh: Edinburgh University Press.

About the Applicability of Combining Implicit Crowdsourcing and Language Learning for the Collection of NLP Datasets.

Verena Lyding[1], Lionel Nicolas[1], Alexander König[2]
[1]Eurac Research, Bolzano, Italy, [2]CLARIN ERIC, Utrecht, Netherlands
verena.lyding,lionel.nicolas@eurac.edu, alex@clarin.eu

Abstract

In this article, we present a recent trend of approaches, hereafter referred to as Collect4NLP, and discuss its applicability. Collect4NLP-based approaches collect inputs from language learners through learning exercises and aggregate the collected data to derive linguistic knowledge of expert quality. The primary purpose of these approaches is to improve NLP resources, however sincere concern with the needs of learners is crucial for making Collect4NLP work. We discuss the applicability of Collect4NLP approaches in relation to two perspectives. On the one hand, we compare Collect4NLP approaches to the two crowdsourcing trends currently most prevalent in NLP, namely Crowdsourcing Platforms (CPs) and Games-With-A-Purpose (GWAPs), and identify strengths and weaknesses of each trend. By doing so we aim to highlight particularities of each trend and to identify in which kind of settings one trend should be favored over the other two. On the other hand, we analyze the applicability of Collect4NLP approaches to the production of different types of NLP resources. We first list the types of NLP resources most used within its community and second propose a set of blueprints for mapping these resources to well-established language learning exercises as found in standard language learning textbooks.

Keywords: Crowdsourcing, Language Learning, Natural Language Processing, Language Resources

1. Introduction

The lack of NLP resources or the quality and/or coverage issues of existing ones is a long-standing obstacle that has slowed down the research in NLP for all languages in general, especially for lower-resourced ones. As most NLP resources cannot be obtained in a purely automatic fashion, creating and/or curating them requires human intervention and, accordingly, a key obstacle for the creation of such datasets is the high cost, both temporal and economic. As a result, most efforts to build NLP resources have focused on a limited set of NLP resources for a handful of languages such as English and other widely used languages. In order to tackle this challenge, some efforts have relied on *crowdsourcing* (Howe and others, 2006) to increase the amount of manpower and/or reduce costs.

Indeed, as reCAPTCHA and the Wikipedia initiative have proven, crowdsourcing is a versatile approach that can be successfully applied to overcome challenging tasks that, in most cases, cannot be solved by automatic means and/or require an excessive amount of cost-intensive expert manpower. Crowdsourcing can be applied in many fields, provided that the tasks tackled can be solved by a crowd of people with a compatible skill set. This aspect makes NLP a very apt field of application since, depending on how the task is presented, it can rely on the language skills of any language speaker as a potential crowd to tackle the collection of NLP datasets for the languages spoken nowadays.[1] Efforts aiming at crowdsourcing NLP resources thus started soon after the rise of crowdsourcing back in 2006 (Howe and others, 2006) and have been followed up by numerous efforts over the past 1.5 decades.

In this article, we discuss the recent trend of Collect4NLP-based approaches which collect the inputs provided by language learners to exercises automatically generated from NLP resources and aggregate them in order to derive linguistic knowledge of expert quality (Nicolas et al., 2021) that can be used to update and/or extend NLP resources. In other words, they consider language learners as linguistic experts through a controlled setting designed in the form of language learning exercises and use a large quantity of their inputs to make up for their lower reliability.

First we discuss the applicability of the Collect4NLP approach by comparing it to Crowdsourcing Platform (CP) and Games-With-A-Purpose (GWAPs) based approaches in Section 4, and then present a range of NLP resource types that are compatible with Collect4NLP-based approaches by discussing how the NLP resources could be mapped to exercises in language learning textbooks in Section 5. Before, in Section 2, we overview the state of the art and briefly introduce in Section 3 the key aspects of the Collect4NLP approaches. We discuss future work and conclude in Section 6.

2. Related Works

The related works include the different trends of crowdsourcing approaches used to collect NLP datasets. As such, the relevant state of the art is composed of the three aforementioned trends (CP-based, GWAP-based and Collect4NLP-based approaches) and single efforts that do not fit in any of the three trends.

CP-based crowdsourcing approaches are the ones most commonly explored since crowdsourcing came into the NLP landscape. They rely on dedicated platforms in

[1]Even though linguistic skills can vary among people.

Proceedings of the 2nd Workshop on Novel Incentives in Data Collection from People @LREC2022, pages 46–57

which users perform tasks and are rewarded for it, such as the Amazon Mechanical Turk[2] (AMT), Clickworker[3] or CrowdFactory[4]. In general, the reward on crowdsourcing platforms is a financial compensation of some sorts. In addition, a few crowdsourcing platforms exist, which base their work on a purely altruistic or educational motivation of their volunteers, in the spirit of Citizen Science, such as e.g. Zooniverse[5] or Distributed Proofreaders [6]. Relevant examples of efforts of this trend are, among many others, efforts to collect and transcribe speech corpora (Callison-Burch and Dredze, 2010; Evanini et al., 2010), to carry out word-sense disambiguation (Biemann, 2013) and named entity annotation (Finin et al., 2010; Lawson et al., 2010; Ritter et al., 2011), to create parallel corpora (Zaidan and Callison-Burch, 2011; Post et al., 2012) or to translate WordNets (Ganbold et al., 2018).
GWAP-based approaches mostly started after 2010 and became a trend sufficiently developed and specific to motivate the organization of a regular series of dedicated 'Games and NLP' workshops collocated with NLP conferences.[7] Some of the most well-known GWAP-efforts concern the annotation of anaphoras (Chamberlain et al., 2008; Poesio et al., 2012; Poesio et al., 2013), lexico-semantic associations between words (Lafourcade, 2007), knowledge rules (Rodosthenous and Michael, 2016), syntactic dependency relations (Fort et al., 2014; Guillaume et al., 2016a) or annotation of text-segmentation (Madge et al., 2017), but GWAPs have also been used for other specific subjects such as e.g. the labelling of speech data for language recognition tasks (Cieri et al., 2021).
Collect4NLP-based approaches started to be more intensively explored in the context of a European network project called enetCollect COST Action (European Network for Combining Language Learning with Crowdsourcing Techniques) started in 2017 and completed in 2021 (Nicolas et al., 2020). This project fostered the development of numerous efforts to combine language learning and crowdsourcing to create lexical knowledge or semantic relations between words (Rodosthenous et al., 2019; Lyding et al., 2019; Rodosthenous et al., 2020; Millour et al., 2019; Smrz, 2019; Araneta et al., 2020; Arhar Holdt et al., 2021) or knowledge about idioms (Eryiğit et al., 2022). To our knowledge related research prior to enetCollect is very limited and just includes a few efforts in order to collect translations (von Ahn, 2013), part-of-speech annotations (Sangati et al., 2015) and syntactic dependencies (Hladká et al., 2014) or is related only to the exercise generation part of the paradigm, such as works by (Greene et al., 2004) or (Pilán and Johansson, 2013).
The state of the art also includes crowdsourcing efforts that do not fit well in any of the three trends. With respect to this "varia" group, the state of the art includes, among others, efforts to collect sentiment annotations (Funk et al., 2018), spelling errors (Tachibana and Komachi, 2016) and speech data (Mollberg et al., 2020).

[2]https://www.mturk.com/
[3]https://www.clickworker.com
[4]https://www.cloudfactory.com/
[5]https://www.zooniverse.org/
[6]https://www.pgdp.net
[7]https://gamesandnlp.com/past-workshops/

3. Collect4NLP in a Nutshell

The umbrella term Collect4NLP stands for *Combining Language Learning with Crowdsourcing Techniques for NLP dataset collection* and includes all approaches implementing an implicit crowdsourcing paradigm (Nicolas et al., 2020). This paradigm states that ***IF*** *an NLP dataset can be used to generate language learning exercises* ***THEN*** *the answers to these exercises can be used to enhance the NLP dataset.*
The paradigm frames a synergy between NLP stakeholders and language learners, resulting from the fact that, on an abstract level, both groups perform similar types of actions: creating and curating a language model. Indeed, while the former create, curate and use a language model in the form of a digital NLP dataset that "teaches" a computer program how to process and produce language content, the latter create, curate and use a language model in the form of personal knowledge allowing them to process and produce language data. By channeling through crowdsourcing the learners' efforts to complete exercises that are automatically-generated from NLP resources, the learners formulate, as a "side-effect" of the learning activity, linguistically-motivated choices and decisions. Those can be used as a (potentially noisy) source of data for the enhancement of NLP resources. In other words, this paradigm considers learners as linguists of lower reliability. Instead of consulting expert linguists on a linguistic question, the paradigm suggests to combine the implicit "judgements" of several learners to answer the same linguistic question.
As demonstrated in Nicolas et al. (2021) for the use-case of enhancing a lexical network for Romanian with synonyms, aggregation mechanisms can make up for the lower reliability of learner data by combining a larger quantity of data. This way by aggregating the inputs of multiple learners to a same set of questions linguistic knowledge of expert quality can be created.
Such aggregation mechanisms work best if the inputs crowdsourced from the learners are as simple as possible. If an exercise allows one to, directly or indirectly, deduce a yes/no judgement from the learner (e.g. *Is 'food' a common noun?*) then we would assume that in most cases[8] the reliability of the learners' answers will range from 50% (random answers) to 100% (correct answer). This implies that each single learner answer, even the weakest ones with 51% reliability, will contribute to reaching statistical certainty. In other words, provided that a sufficient number of answers to the

[8]effects of language interference like 'false friends' aside

same yes/no question can be collected, deriving the correct answer by cross-matching multiple learner judgements is statistically achievable.

4. Weaknesses and Strengths across the Three Trends of Approaches

In this section, we discuss how the three trends of crowdsourcing approaches compare to one another with respect to the following partly interrelated aspects: crowd motivation, crowd size, crowd involvement, crowdsourcing rate, crowdsourcing quality, and crowdsourcing costs. The crowd size and involvement as well as the crowdsourcing rate and quality are the key variables influencing the amount of data that can be crowdsourced for each trend, if successfully applied. Indeed, the larger the crowd involved and the higher the crowdsourcing quality and resulting crowdsourcing rate the greater will be the amount of data that can be crowdsourced in a certain amount of time.

The crowd motivation and crowdsourcing costs describe the core conditions that have to be met to set up approaches of each crowdsourcing trend and keep them running. The crowd motiviation describes the preconditions and incentives for a crowdsourcing trend to work, while the crowdsourcing costs discuss the technical and pragmatical requirements that have to be fulfilled to put a crowdsourcing trend into practice.

The detailed comparison relies on the practical experience we accumulated in researching Collect4NLP approaches while also keeping track of the state of the art of the two other trends.

We conclude this section by an overall discussion of the comparable aspects and individual strengths and weaknesses of each of the trends in relation to the others.

4.1. Crowd Motivation

The major factor for any crowdsourcing initiative to be successful is the incentive it provides for a crowd to participate. The three trends we are looking at provide substantially different incentives for participation.

CP. Crowdsourcing platforms attract their crowdworkers by a financial award for each crowdsourcing action that is a small amount of money for each completed HIT (Human Intelligence Task). Poesio et al. (2017) report that rewards are usually fairly small in the range from 0.01 - 0.20 US $ per HIT, depending on the complexity of the task. The higher the award the higher the motivation to participate.

GWAP. GWAP approaches aim to attract a crowd by offering some fun or interesting game-like interaction which at the time of game-playing is collecting data. GWAPs use different gamification features like interaction with other players, leaderboards, speed, level progression and badge systems. This way they aim to attract different types of game players, like *socializers*, *achievers* or *players* (Tondello et al., 2016). The more satisfying or addictive the game experience the higher the motivation to participate.

Collect4NLP. Collect4NLP approaches aim to integrate crowdsourcing activities with a language learning service. Thus the incentive for a crowd of people to participate is their desire or need to improve their language skills. The more effective and engaging the language learning experience the higher the motivation to participate.

4.2. Crowd Size

Concerning crowd size we have to distinguish between the overall size of the crowd that can be targeted by a set of approaches and the effective subset of the target crowd that we might be able to reach and involve for each trend (see Section 4.3 on crowd involvement).

CP. Due to being a paid service and related legal and tax regulations the crowd targeted by crowd platforms is limited to legal adults. For the same reasons, some platforms such as Amazon Mechanical Turk (AMT) require their users to be tax payers of a specific country. Finally, depending on the crowdsourcing task a certain level of language skills or a limitation to speakers of a specific mother tongue might be imposed by the task provider. Overall, CP-based approaches tend to apply stronger selection criteria on their crowd than GWAPs and Collect4NLP which limits the size of the crowd but safeguards crowdsourcing quality (see Section 4.5).

GWAP. The target group for GWAPs comprises theoretically everyone who has access to a computer device. GWAPs particularly target a public that is interested in playing games which is known to be huge and rapidly growing.[9] In 2008, von Ahn and Dabbish (2008) stated that according to a report of the Entertainment Software Association 'more than 200 million hours are spent each day playing computer and video games in the U.S.'. However, it has to be considered that most GWAPs are not comparable to modern video games in terms of their user experience but rather offer a user-friendly task design with some gamification features.[10] As with CPs, for language-related GWAPs the size of the target crowd is also limited by the required language skills of its users though the pre-selection of the crowd is less strict than for CPs.

Two of the most successful GWAPs for creating NLP resources are Jeux-de-mots (Lafourcade and Nathalie, 2020) and Phrase Detectives (Chamberlain et al., 2016). Over six years, more than 2700 active users have created an annotated corpus of 302,224 tokens in Phrase Detectives, and over a period of 13 years around 1.47 million games of Jeux-de-Mots have been played.

Collect4NLP. Similarly to GWAPs, the size of the crowds that can potentially be involved in a Collect4NLP-based effort are enormous as the target

[9] `https://www.researchandmarkets.com/reports/5546908/gaming-market-global-industry-trends-share`

[10] Jurgens and Navigli (2014) observe that 'current games are largely text-based and closely resemble traditional annotation tasks' (see also Section 4.3)

group, in principle, extends to all people interested in learning a language. Indeed, a report from the European Commission (2012) states that 21% of the Europeans aged over 14 years, which amounts to about 90 million people, are actively learning a language. Given that a good share of them should have access to online tools the target group theoretically amounts to several million people.

4.3. Crowd Involvement

The crowd involvement depends on the outreach to recruit a crowd and the duration of their participation to the crowdsourcing effort, also called user retention.

CP. For CP-based approaches, the outreach to a crowd is managed by the platforms themselves. CPs usually have large user bases and effective mechanisms to promote tasks. While the average participation time per week can considerably vary among crowdworkers, studies have proven that the involvement in crowdsourcing activities on CPs is mid-to-long term (more than several months or years) for more than half of the crowdworkers.[11] Given that participation is financially driven, the size of the participating crowd can be adjusted by increasing the provided budget.

GWAP. With respect to the outreach to participants, GWAP-based approaches usually rely on specialized channels of dissemination (e.g. specialized mailing lists) and social media campaigns. The duration of the crowd's participation to GWAP approaches is limited by the time the game offered remains attractive to the users and some GWAPs managed to find some very loyal users (e.g. Poesio et al. (2012)). This attractiveness aspect can be a fairly challenging one to tackle as it requires researchers to formulate and provide linguistic tasks in a joyful manner while competing with immense amounts of games devised primarily for the purpose of entertainment and often with a much higher development and promotional budget. We therefore often observe that even highly elaborated and promoted GWAPs are no longer used or available after some time.

Collect4NLP. With respect to the outreach to a crowd of language learners we have to distinguish two scenarios: outreach to learners for participating in prototypical Collect4NLP learning applications and outreach to learners for using a fully-fledged learning solution that integrates Collect4NLP approaches. The first case relies on promotion campaigns and is comparable to the outreach efforts for GWAPs. The second case would be more comparable to the promotion of CPs as stable programs that provide a specific service to its users. While several efforts of the first type have been created in the past years, until now no large-scale application of Collect4NLP approaches in full-grown or commercial language learning applications exists. As prototypical efforts have shown (cf. e.g., Lyding et al. (2019; Nicolas et al. (2021)) a crowd of users can be successfully attracted for an experiment but this does not guarantee that a substantial part of the crowd will continue being active beyond the duration of an experimental period of a few weeks. This is likely due to the limited learning value any prototypical application can offer. It logically follows from this observation that the involvement of a bigger crowd of learners presupposes the systematic integration of Collect4NLP approaches into a full-grown (and possibly established) language learning platform. Once this can be achieved (see Section 4.6) the outreach to learners and their retention should become very feasible, as the growing business of online language learning solutions shows (see e.g. the growth of DuoLingo[12], Babbel[13] and Busuu[14] over the past years).

4.4. Crowdsourcing Rate

In addition to the size of the crowd that can be reached, the crowdsourcing rate, that is the rate of return for the different crowdsourcing trends, depends on two factors: (1) the ratio between the user's time investment and the data crowdsourced, and (2) the aggregation factor to derive reliable results from crowdsourced data. Accordingly, one hour of activity of a crowd of 20 people can have a greatly different crowdsourcing revenue for each of the different crowdsourcing trends.

CP. CP-based approaches allocate almost all of the user's time to crowdsourcing tasks. Excluded are only some training tasks to prepare the user or occasionally testing to evaluate the reliability of the users or to select a subset of them. Given that training sessions or selection tests are usually unpaid[15] the ratio of crowdsourcing is close to 100%. Also, crowdworkers are selected and evaluated (see Section 4.5), therefore the aggregation factor is expected to be rather low to derive a meaningful result, though task-dependent. The rate of return for CP-based approaches is very high.

GWAP. GWAP-based approaches are comparable to CP-based approaches with respect to both the crowdsourcing ratio and the aggregation factor. The reliability of crowdplayers is difficult to estimate a priori. On the one hand, other than paid crowdworkers (cf. Eickhoff and de Vries (2013)) crowdplayers have no reason to cheat as they do not earn money with the activity. On the other hand, nothing might restrain them from cheating, as players have less to lose in case they would be expelled from the activity. The rate of return for GWAP-based approaches is high.

[11] International Labour Organization (2018) report that '56 per cent of survey respondents had performed crowdwork for more than a year; 29 per cent had crowdworked for more than three years'.

[12] `https://www.duolingo.com/`

[13] `https://www.babbel.com/`

[14] `https://www.busuu.com/`

[15] International Labour Organization (2018) report that 'On average, workers spent 20 minutes on unpaid activities for every hour of paid work, searching for tasks, taking unpaid qualification tests, researching clients to mitigate fraud and writing reviews.

Collect4NLP. Collect4NLP-based approaches need to work on top of a proper language learning service as the language learning offer is the incentive for the crowd of users to participate. As such, learning services need to ensure a reliable feedback for most tasks they send to their users while they can only crowdsource data from users for a smaller fraction of the tasks. This only allows for a very low crowdsourcing ratio of ideally less than 10% which could be increased by intelligent strategies for deriving meaningful feedback from less reliable source data. Also, language learners are expected to be less reliable than both (mother tongue) crowdworkers and crowdplayers which requires a higher aggregation factor and leads to a lower crowdsourcing rate for Collect4NLP-based approaches as compared to CP and GWAP.

4.5. Crowdsourcing Quality

The quality of NLP data collected by any crowdsourcing trend depends on the linguistic expertise of its crowd as well as on the performance profiling of each member of the crowd. The estimated proficiency and performance of the crowd will determine the aggregation factor and thus in return strongly impact the crowdsourcing rate as described above.

CP. CP-based approaches usually target L1 speakers or proficient L2 speakers. In addition, often pre-tests or intermediate testing is performed to identify and exclude low-performing crowdworkers.

GWAP. GWAP-based approaches also usually target proficient L1 or L2 speakers. They sometimes request an initial training phase to learn how the GWAP works (cf. e.g. Fort et al. (2020), Chamberlain et al. (2016)) but rarely exclude participants through pre-testing .

Collect4NLP. Collect4NLP-based approaches target language learners which are typically composed of lesser proficient L1 speakers improving their mother tongues and mostly L2 speakers learning foreign languages. As such, the overall linguistic expertise of the crowds targeted by Collect4NLP approaches can greatly vary, and requires the continuous profiling of the performances of their participants in order to give different weight to the answers of different learners when aggregating the data crowdsourced from them.

4.6. Crowdsourcing Costs

One of the major advantages of crowdsourcing for data collection is the expectedly lower cost as compared to traditional contractual work. Still costs occur for any crowdsourcing initiative to be set up and kept running.

CPs. On the one hand, CP-based approaches come with costs for paying each HIT performed by the crowdworkers. On the other hand, infrastructure costs for setting up a CP-based crowdsourcing activity are very low. Crowdsourcing platforms have been around for almost two decades now (e.g. the AMT was launched in 2005) and have received a great deal of attention ever since. Accordingly, a rather diversified set of platforms with varying characteristics have been developed, tested and used. Therefore, there exist clear solutions to define tasks and process the data crowdsourced that anybody can rely on.

GWAP. In GWAP-based approaches no costs have to be foreseen for paying the crowd, however compared to CP-based approaches less ready-to-use infrastructure is available which leads to higher development costs. GWAP-approaches can rely on a number of freely available code repositories and libraries such as PythonGameLibraries[16] in order to implement the gaming aspects of their approaches. Also, a growing number of previous efforts such as Fort et al. (2020) and Guillaume et al. (2016b) have made their code freely available. However, as different GWAPs usually target very specific and varying crowdsourcing tasks and require different solutions for the processing of the data crowdsourced, the creation of any new GWAP comes with considerable development costs[17].

Collect4NLP. As a recent research trend, Collect4NLP has no generic reference code repositories or libraries to rely on at present, even though code repositories of several prototypes such as in Lyding et al. (2019) and Araneta et al. (2020) are made freely available. This means that the development of Collect4NLP approaches is open-ended and challenging and corresponding development costs are currently still high. In addition, even though the automatic generation of language learning exercises has been researched in numerous CALL efforts, most past efforts have primarily focused on textual data in which part of a textual content is removed and learners are asked to fill a gap (cf. e.g. Knoop and Wilske (2013; Lee et al. (2019)) but not on a wider variety of different types of content provided by NLP resources (e.g. lexical networks). As such, also the generation of exercises is an open research challenge that comes with considerable costs.

4.7. Which Trend to Favor over the Others?

The detailed discussion of the three trends of approaches demonstrates that each trend has its particular strengths and none of them truly dominates the other two. When undertaking a new initiative to crowdsource NLP datasets, and more generally speaking when envisioning the future of crowdsourcing NLP datasets we should therefore carefully consider what each trend has to offer, and which investments it requires.

CP-based approaches are the most established and most reliable solution, be it in terms of crowd involvement, crowdsourcing rate or crowdsourcing quality. They are the most seamless way to start a new crowdsourcing project as they rely on established service infrastructures (e.g. AMT) and the crowd size is easily scalable as long as financial means are available to pay for the

[16]`https://wiki.python.org/moin/PythonGameLibraries`

[17]Poesio et al. (2013) indicate a total of around 100,000 US $ of development costs for Phrase Detectives which allowed to annoatate 162,000 complete tokens in three years.

crowdworkers. Leaving ethical issues aside (Fort et al. (2011), Schmidt (2013)), the major drawback of CP-based approaches are their continuous costs.
GWAPs and Collect4NLP-based approaches have the potential to greatly reduce costs in the long term, as the crowd is participating due to motivations other than financial ones. However, the challenge of these approaches is to satisfy the expectations of the crowd, be it in terms of fun in playing games or progress in learning a language. For GWAPs this means creating games that live up to today's gaming standards, while for Collect4NLP-based approaches an integration with existing effective language learning solutions would be desirable. Creating effective solutions requires considerable research and development efforts. As mentioned above, little programming frameworks and tools for the creation of GWAP-based and Collect4NLP-based approaches exist, and for Collect4NLP also the mechanisms for generating exercises and aggregating potentially flawed learner responses still have to be explored and defined. If these challenges can be overcome, for both trends large crowds could be involved. This would also allow to make up for the expected lower crowdsourcing rate and lower crowdsourcing quality, in particular in relation to Collect4NLP-based approaches.
We conclude that for achieving short-term results of reasonable scope CP-based approaches are the safest and most economical choice. At the same time, we see a strong need for advancing research and development efforts on GWAP-based and Collect4NLP-based approaches in order to work towards sustainable solutions in the long term, provided that such approaches could rely on an immense crowd of unpaid contributors and thus bear a much greater and ethically less problematic potential to advance NLP resource creation.

5. Applicability of the Approach for Different Types of NLP Resources

In order to demonstrate how the Collect4NLP approach could be applied to different types of NLP resources we started by looking for a reference set of common language resource types. After some searching we ended up at the CLARIN Resource Families (CRF) (Fišer et al., 2018), which we decided to be a suitable reference set. The CRF are a manually curated set of collections of linguistic resources (and tools, but those are not relevant for our approach) grouped into so-called families. They provide an overview of the resources available in the CLARIN infrastructure and beyond and thus constitute a de facto standard of the current state-of-the-art of NLP resources in Europe. They have been very popular with researchers, because they adhere to certain quality standards and come with brief descriptions and the most important metadata, such as resource size, text sources, time periods, annotations and licences as well as links to download pages or concordancers.
The CRF distinguish three coarse groups of resources: corpora, lexical resources and tools, of which the first two are relevant for our case. The groups are subdivided into more fine grained categories as displayed for corpora and lexical resources in Table 1

Corpora	Lexical resources
Computer-mediated communication corpora	Lexica
Corpora of academic texts	Dictionaries
Historical corpora	Conceptual Resources
L2 learner corpora	Glossaries
Literary corpora	Wordlists
Manually annotated corpora	
Multimodal corpora	
Newspaper corpora	
Parallel corpora	
Parliamentary corpora	
Reference corpora	
Spoken corpora	

Table 1: NLP resources in the CRF

5.1. Tasks in NLP Resource Collection

The corpora and lexical resources listed among the CRF cover a wide range of datasets. They differ both in terms of their type of content as well as, and partly related to it, in their basic data characteristics and the annotation layers applied to them.
For corpora the most prevailing characteristics are contemporary and written data and the most prevalent annotations are basic processing including:

- tokenisation
- lemmatisation
- PoS/MSD-tagging
- syntactic parsing (partly).

For lexical resources the following data entries and annotations are most common:

- lemmas
- word forms
- basic morphological information
- semantic relations
- usage examples.

These characteristics translate into a set of tasks for creating or curating NLP resources, such as *'detecting word boundaries'*, *'assigning grammatical categories to words'*, *'linking words by semantic relations'*, *'creating word definitions'*, etc.
These tasks are usually carried out intentionally by experts or instructed laymen in order to create NLP resources. However, we claim that the Collect4NLP approach allows to shift part of these tasks to language learners. This requires to provide them with a meaningful learning exercise, whose completion produces the required type of data as a side effect.

Exercise	Annotation
'Odd-one out'	semantic relation
Synonyms	semantic relation
Antonyms	semantic relation
Forming word groups	semantic relation
Identify words	headword selection
Assign grammar category	part-of-speech tagging
Filling the gap	part-of-speech tagging

Table 2: Language exercises and related annotations

In the following subsections we first look into common language learning exercises, and second outline a number of blueprints for how language learning exercises can be combined with NLP resource creation tasks.

5.2. Relevant Exercises for Collect4NLP

To get an overview of the types of exercises that are commonly used in language learning we investigated a number of language learning books. Assuming that established exercise types are effective and meaningful for language learning we created a list of those exercises that could serve for crowdsourcing purposes. The resulting collection (see Annex A) is, obviously, not an exhaustive list, but we tried to get a more diverse sample by looking at books from various publishers, courses for various languages and various types of books (e.g. full language course, exercise book).
While looking at the exercises we kept in mind which annotation tasks we aim to complete and grouped the exercises accordingly (see Table 2).
Hereafter, we explain for a number of exercises how they can be used to generate or correct NLP resources.

5.3. Blueprints

The purpose of the following blueprints is to provide examples of pairs of NLP resources and language learning exercises and to show how they can be combined to both serve a language learning need and to crowdsource NLP data. The full list of blueprints is found in a related technical report[18].

5.3.1. 'Odd-One Out' and 'Find the Companion'

One classic exercise type consists of a list of words of which the learner has to select the 'odd-one out'. The exercise is designed such that all words apart from one have the same semantic property (e.g. *'days of the week'*). In order to correctly identify the one word that is different the learner has to understand the meaning of the different words. Figure 1 gives an example of this type of exercise for learners of Italian.
The NLP resources that such an exercise could be linked to are conceptual lexica or wordnets (see CRF[19])

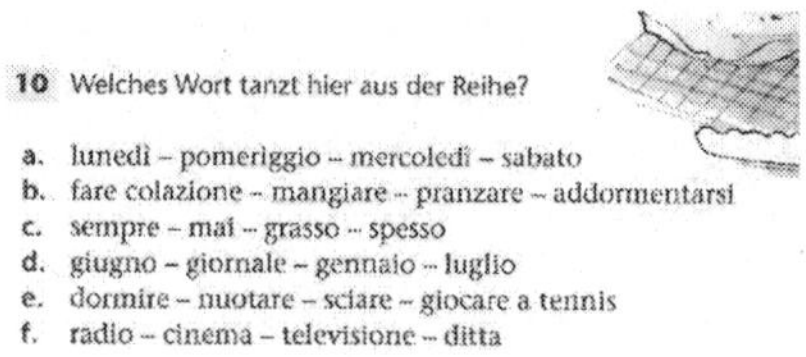

Figure 1: Find the 'odd-one out'

that encode hyponymy relations. For example, 'bulldog', 'labrador' and 'poodle' are all hyponyms of the hypernym 'dog breed', while 'sparrow' is not.
Blueprint: A language learning exercise could automatically be generated from a conceptual network by extracting several hyponyms of any relevant hypernym[20] and by putting any word that is not among the hyponyms in the middle. When used in language learning the answers given by a number of learners can be used to verify or discard some of the hyponym relations encoded in the resource.
A similar, but slightly different exercise type is the 'find the companion' scenario. It provides a list of words to the learner among which they have to match those pairs of words that have the same meaning. Figure 2 shows an example of this type of exercise for Dutch.

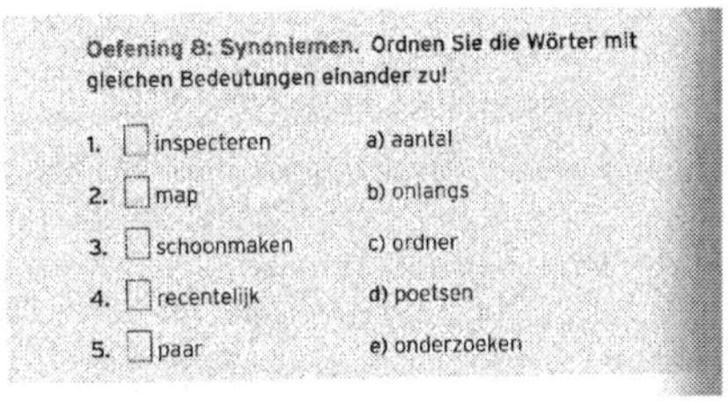

Figure 2: Find the 'companion'

Also here, the NLP resources that such an exercise could be linked to are conceptual lexica or wordnets given that they encode synonymy relations.
Blueprint: A number of synonyms are taken from the wordnet together with words that are suspected to have a similar meaning. Students are presented with the words and have to match the synonyms. If the suspected synonyms are matched a lot of the time this can be taken to mean they are indeed synonyms.

5.3.2. Identify Words in String

Another common type of exercise asks the learners to identify existing words within the target language. Commonly this exercise takes the form of a word grid where the student has to find a certain number of words, see Figure 3 for an example for Italian. Another way is to present the learner with just a very long string that

[18]see `https://enetcollect.net/ilias/goto.php?target=file_1214_download&client_id=enetcollect` for a more comprehensive list

[19]`https://clarin.eu/resource-families/lexical-resources-conceptual-resources`

[20]Relevance will be determined in relation to the learners' level and their learning target, e.g. vocabulary acquisition related to *'food and cooking'*.

contains the words to be identified, see Figure 4 for an example for Dutch.

Was wird Nicoletti zum Essen zubereiten? Finden Sie sechs passende Wörter!

R	B	S	C	A	R	I	F	T	P
A	I	M	O	F	A	S	U	U	R
B	S	E	L	A	E	T	N	O	O
E	T	H	I	C	U	N	G	I	S
G	E	L	A	T	O	A	H	P	C
K	C	O	R	L	P	O	I	E	I
A	C	E	S	A	R	U	G	C	U
E	A	R	I	S	O	T	T	O	T
T	R	A	M	E	Z	I	P	B	T
I	F	R	A	G	O	L	E	J	O

Figure 3: Find words in a grid

As can be seen from the two examples provided, often these exercises constrain the possible words by explicitly stating a semantic domain that they should belong to as in Figure 3, but that is not always the case.

Oefening 6: Verborgen woorden. Finden Sie in der Buchstabenschlange elf versteckte Wörter, die mit „Polizeiarbeit" zu tun haben!

a s w a p e n r f t p o l i t i e a c d r a n z n m a o m o g e w e l d

s m a l m n s c h a d u w e n d d l p o k a a s m i s d a a d o t r u i

p r w c h r r c h m o o r d e s n d d s p a a v o o n d e r z o e k a n

e a r r e s t e r e n o k a r e c h e r c h e k l i j k d r a a l a b b z k

Figure 4: Find words in a string

Such a type of exercise could be used on an annotated text corpus that has been tokenized/lemmatized automatically. The learner input can confirm the results produced by the NLP pipeline by ensuring that it has detected the right words or word forms. For such a setup, one would need the more generic exercises like in figure 4 and not the domain-specific ones. Likewise this exercise type could also be linked again to "word-based" NLP resources like dictionaries and lexica and could help, for example, to confirm possible neologisms that have been pre-identified by an NLP pipeline. If a certain number of learners find these words in the exercise, it can be assumed that they are actual words.

Blueprint: A number of potential words are taken from a) an annotated corpus, which has been tokenized/lemmatized or b) a dictionary where they have been added as neologisms by an NLP pipeline. These possible words are then inserted together with a larger number of "confirmed" words into a word grid or a long string. If most learners also pick out the "new" words they can be considered as actual words.

6. Conclusions and Future Work

We discussed in this article the applicability of the recent trend of Collect4NLP-based crowdsourcing approaches by comparing it to CP-based and GWAP-based approaches with respect to several key aspects and by outlining a first set of blueprints for combining NLP resources with language learning exercises. Our conclusion regarding the relevance and viability of Collect4NLP-based approaches is that they have noticeable advantages over the other two trends with respect to the crowd motivation and accordingly crowd size and crowdsourcing costs. Also, the reported efforts to match language learning exercises with types of NLP datasets suggest that Collect4NLP-based approaches are indeed applicable to several popular types of datasets registered within the CRF. Both analyses indicate the high potential of Collect4NLP-approaches for large-scale and sustainable crowdsourcing efforts, both concerning the crowdsourcing potential as well as concerning the needs of NLP stakeholders curating datasets. At the same time, this new trend also comes with demanding challenges related to researching its mechanisms and integrating them into language learning solutions. In addition to its overall novelty, this may explain why Collect4NLP-approaches have been less researched so far compared to the other two trends.

In terms of future works, as next steps we will discuss our current conclusions on the comparisons discussed in Section 4 with experts in CP- and GWAP-based approaches. Indeed, as our main research expertise lies with Collect4NLP-based approaches our overall vision of the three trends might be biased to some extent and deserves continuous exchange and confrontation with experts of the related communities.

With respect to advancing Collect4NLP-based approaches, our next steps will focus on extending the list of blueprints matching language learning exercises with types of datasets that could be crowdsourced as discussed in Section 5. We foresee to study more textbooks for a wider set of source and target languages, possibly also extending over non-European languages with the intuition that we will encounter other exercises that could be linked to a type of dataset we have not considered yet. With a similar reasoning in mind, we will also explore the types of exercises provided by language learning apps. Last but not least, we intend to perform a finer grained comparison between the types of datasets targeted by previous efforts implementing CP- and GWAP-based approaches in order to evaluate how Collect4NLP-based approaches compare to the other two approaches in relation to dataset coverage.

7. Acknowledgements

This work is based on a virtual mobility grant of COST Action enetCollect (CA16105), supported by COST (European Cooperation in Science and Technology).

8. Bibliographical References

Araneta, M. G., Eryiğit, G., König, A., Lee, J.-U., Luís, A., Lyding, V., Nicolas, L., Rodosthenous, C., and Sangati, F. (2020). Substituto – a synchronous educational language game for simultaneous teaching and crowdsourcing. In *Proceedings of the 9th Workshop on NLP for Computer Assisted Language Learning*, pages 1–9, Gothenburg, Sweden, November. LiU Electronic Press.

Arhar Holdt, Š., Logar, N., Pori, E., and Kosem, I. (2021). "Game of Words": Play the Game, Clean the Database. In *Proceedings of the 14th Congress of the European Association for Lexicography (EURALEX 2021)*, pages 41–49, Alexandroupolis, Greece, July.

Biemann, C. (2013). Creating a system for lexical substitutions from scratch using crowdsourcing. *Language Resources and Evaluation*, 47(1):97–122, Mar.

Callison-Burch, C. and Dredze, M. (2010). Creating speech and language data with amazon's mechanical turk. In *Proceedings of the NAACL HLT 2010 Workshop on Creating Speech and Language Data with Amazon's Mechanical Turk*, pages 1–12. Association for Computational Linguistics.

Chamberlain, J., Poesio, M., and Kruschwitz, U. (2008). Phrase detectives: A web-based collaborative annotation game. In *Proceedings of the International Conference on Semantic Systems (I-Semantics 08)*, pages 42–49.

Chamberlain, J., Poesio, M., and Kruschwitz, U. (2016). Phrase detectives corpus 1.0 crowdsourced anaphoric coreference. In *Proceedings of the Tenth International Conference on Language Resources and Evaluation (LREC'16)*, pages 2039–2046, Portorož, Slovenia, May. European Language Resources Association (ELRA).

Cieri, C., Fiumara, J., and Wright, J. (2021). Using games to augment corpora for language recognition and confusability. In *Proc. Interspeech 2021*, pages 1887–1891.

Eickhoff, C. and de Vries, A. P. (2013). Increasing cheat robustness of crowdsourcing tasks. *Information Retrieval*, 16:121–137.

Eryiğit, G., Şentaş, A., and Monti, J. (2022). Gamified crowdsourcing for idiom corpora construction. *Natural Language Engineering*, page 1–33.

European Commission, D.-G. f. C. (2012). Europeans and their languages. Special eurobarometer 386 report, Survey conducted by TNS Opino & Social, and co-ordinated by the European Commission.

Evanini, K., Higgins, D., and Zechner, K. (2010). Using amazon mechanical turk for transcription of non-native speech. In *Proceedings of the NAACL HLT 2010 Workshop on Creating Speech and Language Data with Amazon's Mechanical Turk*, pages 53–56. Association for Computational Linguistics.

Finin, T., Murnane, W., Karandikar, A., Keller, N., Martineau, J., and Dredze, M. (2010). Annotating named entities in twitter data with crowdsourcing. In *Proceedings of the NAACL HLT 2010 Workshop on Creating Speech and Language Data with Amazon's Mechanical Turk*, pages 80–88. Association for Computational Linguistics.

Fišer, D., Lenardič, J., and Erjavec, T. (2018). CLARIN's Key Resource Families. In Nicoletta Calzolari (Conference chair), et al., editors, *Proceedings of the Eleventh International Conference on Language Resources and Evaluation (LREC 2018)*, Miyazaki, Japan, May. European Language Resources Association (ELRA).

Fort, K., Adda, G., and Cohen, K. B. (2011). Last words: Amazon Mechanical Turk: Gold mine or coal mine? *Computational Linguistics*, 37(2):413–420, June.

Fort, K., Guillaume, B., and Chastant, H. (2014). Creating zombilingo, a game with a purpose for dependency syntax annotation. In *Proceedings of the First International Workshop on Gamification for Information Retrieval*, pages 2–6. ACM.

Fort, K., Guillaume, B., Pilatte, Y.-A., Constant, M., and Lefèbvre, N. (2020). Rigor mortis: Annotating MWEs with a gamified platform. In *Proceedings of the 12th Language Resources and Evaluation Conference*, pages 4395–4401, Marseille, France, May. European Language Resources Association.

Funk, C., Tseng, M., Rajakumar, R., and Ha, L. (2018). Community-driven crowdsourcing: Data collection with local developers. In *Proceedings of the Eleventh International Conference on Language Resources and Evaluation (LREC 2018)*.

Ganbold, A., Chagnaa, A., and Bella, G. (2018). Using crowd agreement for wordnet localization. In *Proceedings of the 11th International Conference on Language Resources and Evaluation (LREC-2018)*.

Greene, C., Keogh, K., Koller, T., Wagner, J., Ward, M., and Genabith, J. (2004). Using nlp technology in call. In *Proceedings of the InSTIL/ICALL Symposium on Computer Assisted Learning 2004*.

Guillaume, B., Fort, K., and Lefebvre, N. (2016a). Crowdsourcing complex language resources: Playing to annotate dependency syntax. In *Proceedings of the International Conference on Computational Linguistics (COLING)*, Osaka, Japan.

Guillaume, B., Fort, K., and Lefebvre, N. (2016b). Crowdsourcing complex language resources: Playing to annotate dependency syntax. In *Proceedings of COLING 2016, the 26th International Conference on Computational Linguistics: Technical Papers*, pages 3041–3052, Osaka, Japan, December. The COLING 2016 Organizing Committee.

Hladká, B., Hana, J., and Lukšová, I. (2014). Crowdsourcing in language classes can help natural language processing. In *Second AAAI Conference on Human Computation and Crowdsourcing*.

Howe, J. et al. (2006). The rise of crowdsourcing. *Wired magazine*, 14(6):1–4.

International Labour Organization, I. (2018). Digital labour platforms and the future of work: Towards decent work in the online world. Executive summary, Survey of working conditions conducted by the International Labour Organization, Geneva, Switzerland.

Jurgens, D. and Navigli, R. (2014). It's all fun and games until someone annotates: Video games with a purpose for linguistic annotation. *Transactions of the Association for Computational Linguistics*, 2:449–464.

Knoop, S. and Wilske, S. (2013). Wordgap - automatic generation of gap-filling vocabulary exercises for mobile learning. In *Proceedings of the second workshop on NLP for computer-assisted language learning at NODALIDA 2013*, pages 39–47, Oslo, Norway, May. Linköping Electronic Conference Proceedings, NEALT Proceedings Series.

Lafourcade, M. and Nathalie, L. B. (2020). Game design evaluation of GWAPs for collecting word associations. In *Workshop on Games and Natural Language Processing*, pages 26–33, Marseille, France, May. European Language Resources Association.

Lafourcade, M. (2007). Making people play for lexical acquisition. In *7th Symposium on Natural Language Processing (SNLP 2007)*, Pattaya, Thailand, December.

Lawson, N., Eustice, K., Perkowitz, M., and Yetisgen-Yildiz, M. (2010). Annotating large email datasets for named entity recognition with mechanical turk. In *Proceedings of the NAACL HLT 2010 workshop on creating speech and language data with Amazon's Mechanical Turk*, pages 71–79. Association for Computational Linguistics.

Lee, J.-U., Schwan, E., and Meyer, C. M. (2019). Manipulating the difficulty of C-tests. In *Proceedings of the 57th Annual Meeting of the Association for Computational Linguistics*, pages 360–370, Florence, Italy, July. Association for Computational Linguistics.

Lyding, V., Rodosthenous, C., Sangati, F., ul Hassan, U., Nicolas, L., König, A., Horbacauskiene, J., and Katinskaia, A. (2019). v-trel: Vocabulary trainer for tracing word relations - an implicit crowdsourcing approach. In *Proceedings of the International Conference on Recent Advances in Natural Language Processing (RANLP 2019)*, pages 674–683, Varna, Bulgaria. INCOMA Ltd.

Madge, C., Chamberlain, J., Kruschwitz, U., and Poesio, M. (2017). Experiment-driven development of a gwap for marking segments in text. In *Extended Abstracts Publication of the Annual Symposium on Computer-Human Interaction in Play*, pages 397–404. ACM.

Millour, A., Araneta, M. G., Lazić Konjik, I., Raffone, A., Pilatte, Y.-A., and Fort, K. (2019). Katana and Grand Guru: a Game of the Lost Words (DEMO). In *Proceedings of the ninth Language & Technology Conference*, Poznan, Poland, May.

Mollberg, D. E., Jónsson, Ó. H., orsteinsdóttir, S., Steingrímsson, S., Magnúsdóttir, E. H., and Gunason, J. (2020). Samrómur: Crowd-sourcing data collection for icelandic speech recognition. In *Proceedings of The 12th Language Resources and Evaluation Conference*, pages 3463–3467.

Nicolas, L., Lyding, V., Borg, C., Forăscu, C., Fort, K., Zdravkova, K., Kosem, I., Čibej, J., Holdt, Š. A., Millour, A., et al. (2020). Creating expert knowledge by relying on language learners: a generic approach for mass-producing language resources by combining implicit crowdsourcing and language learning. In *Proceedings of The 12th Language Resources and Evaluation Conference*, pages 268–278.

Nicolas, L., Aparaschivei, L. N., Lyding, V., Rodosthenous, C., Sangati, F., König, A., and Forascu, C. (2021). An experiment on implicitly crowdsourcing expert knowledge about Romanian synonyms from language learners. In *Proceedings of the 10th Workshop on NLP for Computer Assisted Language Learning*, pages 1–14, Online, May. LiU Electronic Press.

Pilán, Ildikó, E. V. and Johansson, R. (2013). Automatic selection of suitable sentences for language learning exercises. In *20 Years of EUROCALL: Learning from the Past, Looking to the Future: 2013 EUROCALL Conference Proceedings*. Dublin: Research-publishing.net.

Poesio, M., Chamberlain, J., Kruschwitz, U., Robaldo, L., and Ducceschi, L. (2012). The phrase detective multilingual corpus, release 0.1. In *Collaborative Resource Development and Delivery Workshop Programme*, page 34.

Poesio, M., Chamberlain, J., Kruschwitz, U., Robaldo, L., and Ducceschi, L. (2013). Phrase detectives: Utilizing collective intelligence for internet-scale language resource creation. *ACM Trans. Interact. Intell. Syst.*, 3(1):3:1–3:44, April.

Poesio, M., Chamberlain, J., and Kruschwitz, U., (2017). *Crowdsourcing*, pages 277–295. Springer, Dordrecht, 06.

Post, M., Callison-Burch, C., and Osborne, M. (2012). Constructing parallel corpora for six indian languages via crowdsourcing. In *Proceedings of the Seventh Workshop on Statistical Machine Translation*, pages 401–409. Association for Computational Linguistics.

Ritter, A., Clark, S., Etzioni, O., et al. (2011). Named entity recognition in tweets: an experimental study. In *Proceedings of the Conference on Empirical Methods in Natural Language Processing*, pages 1524–1534. Association for Computational Linguistics.

Rodosthenous, C. and Michael, L. (2016). A Hybrid

Approach to Commonsense Knowledge Acquisition. In *Proceedings of the 8th European Starting AI Researcher Symposium (STAIRS 2016)*, volume 284, pages 111–122. IOS Press, August.

Rodosthenous, C. T., Lyding, V., König, A., Horbacauskiene, J., Katinskaia, A., ul Hassan, U., Isaak, N., Sangati, F., and Nicolas, L. (2019). Designing a prototype architecture for crowdsourcing language resources. In Thierry Declerck et al., editors, *Proceedings of the Poster Session of the 2nd Conference on Language, Data and Knowledge (LDK 2019), Leipzig, Germany, May 21, 2019*, volume 2402 of *CEUR Workshop Proceedings*, pages 17–23. CEUR-WS.org.

Rodosthenous, C., Lyding, V., Sangati, F., König, A., ul Hassan, U., Nicolas, L., Horbacauskiene, J., Katinskaia, A., and Aparaschivei, L. (2020). Using crowdsourced exercises for vocabulary training to expand conceptnet. In *Proceedings of The 12th Language Resources and Evaluation Conference*, pages 307–316.

Sangati, F., Merlo, S., and Moretti, G. (2015). School-tagging: interactive language exercises in classrooms. In *LTLT@ SLaTE*, pages 16–19.

Schmidt, F. A. (2013). The good, the bad and the ugly: Why crowdsourcing needs ethics. In *2013 International Conference on Cloud and Green Computing*, pages 531–535.

Smrz, P. (2019). Crowdsourcing Complex Associations among Words by Means of A Game. In *Proceedings of CSTY 2019, 5th International Conference on Computer Science and Information Technology.*, volume 9, Dubai, UAE, December.

Tachibana, R. and Komachi, M. (2016). Analysis of english spelling errors in a word-typing game. In *Proceedings of the Tenth International Conference on Language Resources and Evaluation (LREC'16)*, pages 385–390.

Tondello, G. F., Wehbe, R. R., Diamond, L., Busch, M., Marczewski, A., and Nacke, L. E. (2016). The gamification user types hexad scale. In *Proceedings of the 2016 Annual Symposium on Computer-Human Interaction in Play*, CHI PLAY '16, page 229–243, New York, NY, USA. Association for Computing Machinery.

von Ahn, L. and Dabbish, L. (2008). Designing games with a purpose. *Commun. ACM*, 51(8):58–67, aug.

von Ahn, L. (2013). Duolingo: learn a language for free while helping to translate the web. In *Proceedings of the 2013 international conference on Intelligent user interfaces*, pages 1–2. ACM.

Zaidan, O. F. and Callison-Burch, C. (2011). Crowdsourcing translation: Professional quality from non-professionals. In *Proceedings of the 49th Annual Meeting of the Association for Computational Linguistics: Human Language Technologies-Volume 1*, pages 1220–1229. Association for Computational Linguistics.

A. Appendix

Here we will provide a short list of all the exercise types we identified. For more context, including the accompanying blueprints and example pictures we refer to the related technical report[21].

"Odd one out"
Exercise: Students are presented with a list of words with the same semantic property (e.g. days of the week). They have to pick the one word that does not belong with the others, the "odd one out".

Relation: At location
Exercise: The student is presented with pictures of a number of things that belong to a certain location. For example *"Which of these things can be bought in which kind of store?"* The student has to match the product to the store. Or: *"Which of these types of furniture can be found in which room?"* The student has to match the items of furniture to the rooms.

Labelling, text-retrieval
Exercise: *"What are these ads about?"* Students are presented with short texts that they need to connect to a term that is most likely the topic of the text.

Definitions
Exercise: *"Write down the terms for these definitions."* Students are shown short definitions and have to provide the term that is described.

Collocations
Exercise: *"Connect these fragments to form collocations."* Students are presented with a number of typical collocations (e.g. "a flock of sheep"), but they are broken apart and shuffled. The students need to connect the parts to form real collocations.

Gender
Exercise: *"Fill in the correct adjective in the correct form."* Students are presented with a sentence missing an adjective. The adjectives are provided in their base forms. Students have to match the adjective to the right sentence and make sure that it has the right form to agree with the corresponding noun.

Antonyms
Exercise: *"Write down the opposite."* Students are presented with a number of words and have to provide the opposite.

Generic Relations
Exercise: *"Which words belong together?"* Students are presented with a number of words and have to match them into pairs.

[21]see `https://enetcollect.net/ilias/goto.php?target=file_1214_download&client_id=enetcollect` for a more comprehensive list

Synonyms or "find the companion"
Exercise: *"Match the words that mean the same."* Students are presented with a number of words and have to match the ones that have the same meaning.

Identify words
Exercise: *"Find all the words."* Students are presented with a long string of letters or a word grid in which they have to identify a number of words all related to a specific topic.

Orthography
Exercise: *"Read the text and mark all the orthographic mistakes."* Students are presented with a text and have to mark all orthographic mistakes they can spot.

Grammar
Exercise: *"Check the sentences that contain grammatical errors."* Students are presented with a number of sentences and have to mark the ones that contain a grammatical error.

The Influence of Intrinsic and Extrinsic Motivation on the Creation of Language Resources in a Citizen Linguistics Project about Lexicography

Barbara Heinisch
Centre for Translation Studies, University of Vienna, Austria
Porzellangasse 4, 1090 Vienna
barbara.heinisch@univie.ac.at

Abstract

In the field of citizen linguistics, various initiatives are aimed at the creation of language resources by members of the public. To recruit and retain these participants different incentives informed by different motivations, extrinsic and intrinsic ones, play a role at different project stages. Illustrated by a project in the field of lexicography which draws on the extrinsic and/or intrinsic motivation of participants, the complexity of providing the 'right' incentives is addressed. This complexity does not only surface when considering cultural differences and the heterogeneity of the motivations participants might have but also through the changing motivations over time. Here, identifying target groups may help to guide recruitment, retention and dissemination activities. In addition, continuous adaptations may be required during the course of the project to strike a balance between necessary and feasible incentives.

Keywords: Language varieties, citizen science, language resource development, German in Austria

1. Introduction

Data collection from people can take many forms, including the generation, compilation or annotation of language resources by 'the crowd'. The reasons for collecting data from people are manifold, including a lack of available resources or the need for authentic data. The incentives given in these projects range from monetary compensation to encourage members of the public to participate in the creation of language resources to other forms of recognizing the participants' contributions.

In the case of the Austrian variety of the German language, the diversity of the language resources available is still rather low, partially due to non-availability and the low number of speakers, e.g. of regional dialects, partially also due to the variability of the data formats and lack of metadata. Although the Austrian Language Resource Portal (Heinisch and Lušicky, 2020) is a first step to coordinate and to pool language resources produced in Austria, it nevertheless has a strong focus on administrative language. Therefore, it does not reflect the diversity of language resources available, and the linguistic diversity of the German language used in Austria.

Not many language resources in Austria cover language varieties, such as dialects (European Language Resource Coordination, 2019; Hegele *et al.*, 2022). Moreover, language resources in Austrian dialects are either non-existent or of small size, thus representing the small number of speakers of a certain dialect. However, language varieties in general, and dialects in particular, are interesting not only to researchers but also to language technology providers (Zampieri *et al.*, 2020), e.g. those specialized in speech-to-text or speech recognition technologies.

In this regard, several citizen science projects in the field of linguistics tried to fill this gap by collecting communication data from people directly. Some initiatives also aim at collecting dialectal data, e.g. *What's Up, Switzerland?* from the users of chat communication systems (Schweiz forscht, 2021). In these projects, citizen science is usually characterized by unpaid labor. Therefore, the activity of crowdsourcing the generation, preparation and processing of language resources may benefit from the insights gained in the field of citizen science. There is an increasing literature that addresses the motivation of members of the public who contribute to citizen science projects (Moczek, 2019; Raddick *et al.*, 2010).

Therefore, this paper summarizes the different approaches that were used in a linguistic citizen science project aimed at the generation of lexicographical data by members of the public in Austria.

2. Case study: 'Dictionary' creation by citizens

In the following, the case study of the citizen linguistics project 'On everyone's mind and lips – German in Austria' (abbreviated as IamDiÖ in German) is providing an insight into the different incentives employed throughout the project to create and gather language resources in the form of lexicographical entries. Although the resulting 'dictionary' is a language resource of small scale, the characteristic of the language resources developed by 'On everyone's mind and lips – German in Austria' is that they are intended to meet both the researchers' and the participants' needs.

2.1 'Layperson dictionaries'

This project builds on the numerous enterprises of speakers of dialects in Austria to collect and preserve their dialect in form of (online) dictionaries. From a research perspective, 'layperson' dictionaries may not meet the quality criteria for dictionary entries created according to (standardized) lexicographical principles. On the one hand, this makes the data difficult to find and hampers their access, interoperability and re-use (as required by the FAIR principles). On the other hand, since there are no standards that specify orthography for dialects in Austria, for researchers it is also interesting to investigate how people actually write dialect, either with the standard alphabet or with diacritical or phonetic symbols adapted to their needs.

2.2 Needs of researchers and participants

From the researchers' perspective, the aims of IamDiÖ were to increase the accessibility of language resources that reflect the linguistic diversity, namely the different varieties of the German language used in Austria. For this purpose, participants were invited to collect lexemes in different language varieties in German used in Austria. Therefore, IamDiÖ intended to bridge these so-called 'layperson dictionaries' and dictionaries that were created by professional lexicographers.

For this purpose, the participants were familiarized with the basics of lexicography, i.e. especially the compilation and use of dictionaries with a focus on creating lexicographical entries. This should further support participants in acquiring a critical understanding of their language use and attitudes towards German in Austria.

2.3 The community and its prior experience

Based on a literature review and our previous experience in citizen science projects, different strategies were employed to recruit participants. In the beginning the project primarily targeted people interested in the topic and relied on the already established community of citizen linguists who have already contributed to other activities in the project. Members of the IamDiÖ community have already completed at least one of the following tasks: a) the Question of the Month that required participants to come up with their (research) question regarding the topic of German language in Austria. Ideally, they would also engage in searching for an answer to their question with the help of researchers (this is the co-creation strand of the project), b) linguistic treasure hunts to study the Austrian linguistic landscape or c) they created memes with a focus on (regional) dialects in Austria (Heinisch, 2020). Some participants also filled d) comic strips. They were provided with a comic strip consisting of three pictures, in which people of different age and gender talked to each other. Since the speech bubbles in the comic strip were empty, the participants were asked to fill them. To illicit linguistic diversity, they were prompted to complete the bubbles with the language or language variety of their choice. We also told them that correct spelling does not matter. This was especially important since dialects of the German language in Austria are only transmitted orally and do not follow a written standard. Moreover, this should avoid embarrassment if the spelling was not perceived as correct. Following the filling of the speech bubbles, the participants were asked to place their comic strip on a standard-non-standard and closeness-distance coordinate system. The underlying purpose of this exercise was to test the hypothesis that people tend to speak non-standard language, especially dialects with people to whom they have a close(r) relationship and use standard language when talking to people to whom the relationship is more distant.

Here, the motivation to engage in this activity was entertainment and fun, especially for children. However, some children also voiced complaints since they have to do similar things in school, which clearly diminished their motivation to engage in 'school activities' in their leisure time.

2.4 Incentives

Over the course of the project, IamDiÖ used different incentives to recruit participants, retain them or reward them for their contributions, including those targeted at the extrinsic motivation and those focusing on the intrinsic motivation of the participants.

2.4.1 Extrinsic motivation: Citizen Science Award

The Citizen Science Award is an initiative in Austria that encourages researchers running a citizen science project to take part in a nation-wide competition. However, the competition is not between citizen science projects but among the participants within a citizen science project. The competition is organized and coordinated by the OeAD, which is Austria's Agency for Education and Internationalisation, which also invites researchers to be part of the Citizen Science Award and selects the projects for the competition. The selected citizen science projects specify a task for the competition, i.e. how participants can contribute to their project. The researchers also have to define criteria for the evaluation of the participants' contributions in the competition. There are two participant categories, either adult individuals or school classes. The winning adults receive a material prize while winning school classes receive money for school activities (OeAD, 2022). Furthermore, the participating projects were also supported by the OeAD throughout the Citizen Science Award period to attract persons and school classes to participate in the competition.

Since IamDiÖ also participated in the Citizen Science Award 2021, the incentives were already provided by the organizers and clearly targeted at extrinsic motivation, i.e. being the winner and receiving a prize. Therefore, it was important to clearly specify the criteria that were applied for determining the winner in each participating citizen science project. In case of IamDiÖ, the participants were required to create lexicographical entries in the project's 'online dictionary' tool *Wortgut*. To win this competition, the quantity of different lexicographical entries and the quantity of the data provided within each lexicographical entry were key.

The focus was on the quantity of the data provided by the participants since quality control and validation of the provided data was not possible. The wide range of lexemes entered in the tool and the high number of dialects in Austria would have necessitated an expert for each and every dialect and for youth language. Since it was not feasible to check the lexicographical data entered by the participants, IamDiÖ relied on the good intentions of the users. However, a 'reporting button' was provided so that users could report discriminating or offensive content published by other users. Furthermore, users could also

label their own entries as being offensive or as containing profanity.
To emphasize the research aspect in the project, school classes were also asked to submit a research report in which they describe their topic of the lexemes collected, the reason for selecting this topic, their motivation as well as their approach. This research report should help the pupils to reflect on their language use on the one hand and to assess the quality of their lexicographical entries, on the other. This reflects again the main maxim of the project that not only the researchers should benefit from public engagement through the provision of language data and resources but also the participants themselves. While IamDiÖ did not conduct empirical studies to investigate the benefits for the participants, the participants' self-reported benefits were to express themselves and to have fun.
The experience gained during the Citizen Science Award showed that it was possible to reach a large number of people who contribute data to a citizen linguistics project to create language resources. Furthermore, the output was promising. However, the participation in the Citizen Science Award required a lot of preparation and intense communication throughout the competition. Especially at the beginning of the competition, the project team organized workshops and consultation hours to familiarize the participants with both the project itself and the criteria of assessment used in the competition. Moreover, the tool used for the creation of lexicographical entries did not only require the provision of help pages and tutorials but also constant technical support.
During the Citizen Science Award, the participants had only a limited amount of time, namely a couple of months to contribute to the different citizen science projects. After the end of the competition, the projects evaluated the participants' contributions and announced the winner(s) in the two categories 'school classes' and 'adult individuals'. Finally, the engagement of the participating schools and adults in the Citizen Science Award initiative is acknowledged and honored in the form of cash and material prizes during a concluding event. As part of a festive ceremony, the winners receive their awards from the leader of the relevant citizen science project and representatives from the OeAD and the Austrian Ministry of Education, Science and Research.
To sum up, the incentives that are relevant in the Citizen Science Award are therefore a competition and the chance of winning a prize (experiencing appreciation and recognition), having personal contact with researchers (this was mentioned by both participant groups, i.e. teachers and adults) and contributing to the advancement of knowledge in academia. This demonstrates that different motivations may play a role at the same time.
Therefore, the incentives focusing on the intrinsic motivation are addressed in the following.

2.4.2 Intrinsic motivation

The collection of lexicographical entries by members of the public also draws on intrinsic motivation. For example, members of the public interested in language can follow their personal interests when engaging in a citizen linguistics project and can become part of a community. Some participants enter data in the 'online dictionary' to preserve their language (preservation efforts) or to make their language use visible as a means of self-expression and expression of identity. Other factors that play a role are the personal contact with the researchers (which may also have an element of receiving appreciation and prestige), gaining an insight into academia or getting access to resources, infrastructure or knowledge that they would not have otherwise. However, also contributing to a greater good, such as the advancement of knowledge or instigating change can play a role.
Nevertheless, for participant retention some form of appreciation, entertainment or novelty may also be necessary. This can take the form of the 'contributor of the month', who can be any participant that contributed significantly to the project in the previous project month. This does not necessarily have to be the person who contributed the most data. It can also be a person who brought the project to the attention of the mayor, who organized an event or who recruited other participants. Any other form of appreciation, such as small gifts, e.g. presents related to the topic of the project or language resource may also provide an incentive to support a project (also) beyond data collection.

2.5 The resulting language resource

After the Citizen Science Award, the language resource to which the participants contributed contained 2,638 lexicographical entries. Since the users can select between distinct levels of difficulty when entering their data, the completeness of the entries varies. Since the entries are neither moderated nor curated, the language resource is currently only available upon request. However, in the future, after the introduction of data validation steps and after collecting additional data, these will become openly accessible.

3. Discussion

Data collection from people can benefit from the insights gained in citizen science projects since accompanying social science research in citizen science projects sheds light onto the motivations underlying the participation of members of the public in citizen science projects.
Since data collection from people is usually mediated through technology, the aspect of the usability of the system through which participants contribute to a project should not be underestimated. Therefore, in the case of online citizen science, in addition to participant motivation, the usability of technology is of the utmost importance (Nov *et al.*, 2011).

3.1 Target groups

In the IamDiÖ project, we had different target groups, including, broadly speaking, schoolchildren, adolescents, schoolteachers, university students, adults and the elderly having an interest in language. We also learned that not only the needs between these target groups but also within these groups varied significantly. Moreover, the type and the context of participation differed significantly. In the

case of schoolchildren, they may either take part as a school class or individually. This may lead to competition or cooperation either with other students in the class or with other schools.
Identifying and specifying target groups may help to organize and structure the recruitment, retention and dissemination activities in a citizen linguistics project, but the large heterogeneity within the different target groups and the wide range of contexts in which participants may engage in the creation, annotation or processing of language resources cannot be fully anticipated by the researchers during the initial project design phase. Therefore, continuous adaptations may be required during the course of the project itself and it may also be necessary to find a balance between what is necessary and what is feasible.

3.2 Types of incentives

The motivations of the participants in citizen linguistics projects aimed at the creation of language resources may be different and motivations change over time. Therefore, Rotman *et al.* (2014) analyzed the cycle of engagement as well as the associated motivational pivotal points in citizen science projects. According to them, egoism is the initial motivation of both participants and researchers. While participants may want to broaden their horizons and complete an enjoyable activity, researchers cooperate with members of the public to collect large amounts of data or data that would be hard to obtain otherwise. Later in the project, e.g. if a task is completed or a project has ended, the participants reassess their contributions to the project based on their previous experience. In this phase, the initially prevailing motivational factor of egoism may be replaced by collectivism or altruism (Rotman *et al.*, 2012). As the motivation of participants changes over the course of a project, it is crucial to find the appropriate incentives for different stages in the project to sustain participants.
According to Rotman *et al.* (2014), the motivations underlying initial participation in ecological citizen science projects were a) personal interest, such as leisure or hobbies, b) self-promotion, such as social advancement, career progress or reputation, c) self-efficacy, e.g. having an impact on academia and be known to academic researchers in the community as well as d) social responsibility that may be conservation or being proud of one's nation or region. For participant retention, on the other hand, clear shared goals of the academics and the participants are important. Moreover, participants need confirmation that the researchers value their contributions. Other factors are acknowledgement, e.g. in academic papers, or mentorship as well as societal impact in the broad sense, including policy action (Rotman *et al.*, 2014). Therefore, according to Palacin *et al.* (2020), different incentive mechanisms may be used: These can be remuneration, such as micropayments, reputation mechanisms or gamification on the one hand, and non-monetary incentives, such as hedonism-enhancing aspects or social reward, on the other. For initial participation, values that characterize openness to change are crucial. However, in the later project stages and for participant retention, self-transcendence values come into play. The reason for this is that "when extrinsic motivators are self-directed, people will not only perform tasks willingly and enthusiastically but also in a sustained manner" (Palacin *et al.* 2020, 15). To sum up, a focus on rewards as a means of incentives can foster self-enhancement values and therefore lead to a stronger focus on the person itself, and not the project topic at hand. Therefore, during later project stages, retention can be increased by creating ownership of the project among the participants. This can take the form of transparent processes and control by the members of the public.
This is in line with other studies that suggest that extrinsic motivation can help to recruit participants but does fail to retain participants in the long term. Therefore, intrinsic motivation can increase the long-term engagement of participants in a project, for example through providing "experiences of relatedness, capacity building, positive feedback and adapted participation modes" (Triago *et al.*, 2017).
Fischer *et al.* (2021) developed the Nibble-and-Drop Framework to address typical issues regarding recruitment and retention. They differentiate between several types of contributors according to the level of contribution to a project and the duration of participation. Based on five degrees of participation, they categorize participants into 1) initial droppers who sign up to a project but never contribute, 2) nibblers who contribute to a small extent to a project, 3) nibble droppers who contributed to the project before withdrawing from the project after a short period of time, 4) hooked participants who contribute significantly over a longer period of time and 5) hooked droppers who contributed significantly to a project but dropped out after some time. This framework demonstrates that, in some cases, researchers cannot influence the motivation by providing incentives. For example, participants may drop out after they have fulfilled their concrete personal aims. Others might never really commit to a citizen science project but may just engage in 'window shopping' to test whether the project appeals to them.
In addition to all these different motivational factors throughout a citizen science project, also participant demographics and cultural differences play a role. However, addressing these would be beyond the scope of this paper.

3.3 One-time versus regular contributions and superficial versus in-depth contributions

Furthermore, the incentives provided strongly depend on the project's objectives. If a large number of people should be addressed and one-time contributions are sufficient, the incentives may be different from those projects that require repeated contributions of sufficient quality.
Therefore, researchers may differentiate between superficial or in-depth contributions. If a project mainly relies on superficial contributions, i.e. contributions that do not require subject-related, project-related knowledge or knowledge of the academic process and that can be easily completed without providing in-depth explanations and instructions on how to complete the task, then

'crowdsourcing', including monetary incentives and entertainment may suffice. Anonymity may help, i.e. either the participants can stay anonymous, and they do not need to be part of a community and/or the researchers do not engage in personal dialogue with the participants. In this case, the researchers just provide information, e.g. on the website and recruit participants via different platforms, including social media, traditional media or crowdsourcing platforms.

On the other hand, if in-depth contributions are required either by the academics or the participants, then the provision of training and a sense of community may be needed. A community may also result in the necessary (peer) pressure to continue contributing to the project.

While competitions and contests may increase the engagement of some superficial contributors, it may also decrease the motivation of other contributors if they are falling behind too much and are being listed on the bottom of the contributors' list. Therefore, the incentives should also be adjusted to these aspects.

Other aspects that deserve consideration are the mode of participation, which can be online or on site, e.g. in the field as well as the type of communication between researchers and the participants, which can also take place fully online or face-to-face. According to Cappa *et al.* (2020), also online-mediated citizen science projects can benefit from face-to-face interactions between researchers and participants since these can enhance participant motivation. This effect of face-to-face interactions in online-mediated citizen science is most pronounced in older participants.

4. Conclusion

Language resources unfold their potential if they can be re-used. Therefore, the access to, processing and availability of language resources is of major importance to researchers. To get access to or even create language resources, researchers are taking different routes, among these is the engagement of members of the public in the creation or processing of language resources. While data collection from people can take many forms, researchers can get inspiration from citizen science initiatives, also beyond those that are focusing on the creation of language resources when engaging members of the public in collecting language data.

Since the participants in projects aimed at the creation or processing of language resources may be heterogeneous and doing a target group analysis (at different times of the project) to analyze their needs may not be feasible in research projects that are often characterized by limited funding, short project duration and low (personnel) resources for communication.

Therefore, to find a balance between the desired aims and the feasible aims, a small number of different incentives may be offered (from the very beginning or at different project phases) to address different motivations. Some incentives might be targeted at the participants' intrinsic motivation, such as recognition or acknowledgement, while other incentives might address extrinsic motivation, such as competition or monetary compensation.

To conclude, each project may define success and active participation differently. Therefore, there is no one-size-fits-all incentive for participants in citizen linguistics projects. The selection of incentives depends on the project and its objectives. Nevertheless, incentives that focus on extrinsic motivation can help to recruit participants and incentives that target intrinsic motivation can help to retain participants for a longer period of time. Depending on the aim of the language resource project that involves members of the public also the expression of one's identity through language and making their 'speech' heard may be important aspects to be considered when providing incentives.

5. Acknowledgements

This work has been partly funded by the Austrian Science Fund (FWF): TCS 57-G.

6. Bibliographical References

Cappa, F., Laut, J., Nov, O., Giustiniano, L. and Porfiri, M. (2016) Activating social strategies: Face-to-face interaction in technology-mediated citizen science. *Journal of environmental management*, 182, 2016: 10.1016/j.jenvman.2016.07.092.

European Language Resource Coordination (2019) ELRC White Paper. Why Language Data Matters. http://www.lr-coordination.eu/sites/default/files/ELRC_Conference/ELRCWhitePaper.pdf.

Fischer, H., Cho, H. and Storksdieck, M. (2021) Going Beyond Hooked Participants: The Nibble-and-Drop Framework for Classifying Citizen Science Participation. *Citizen Science: Theory and Practice*, 6, 2021: 10.5334/cstp.350.

Hegele, S., Heinisch, B., Popp, A., Marheinecke, K., Rios, A., Gromann, D. *et al.* (2022) European Language Equality. https://european-language-equality.eu/wp-content/uploads/2022/03/ELE___Deliverable_D1_16__Language_Report_German_.pdf.

Heinisch, B. (2020) Developing Language Resources with Citizen Linguistics in Austria – A Case Study. In Fiumara, J., Cieri, C., Liberman, M. and Callison-Burch, C. (eds), Citizen Linguistics in Language Resource Development (CLLRD 2020) Proceedings. European Language Resources Association (ELRA), pp. 7–14.

Heinisch, B. and Lušicky, V. (2020) The Austrian Language Resource Portal for the Use and Provision of Language Resources in a Language Variety by Public Administration – a Showcase for Collaboration between Public Administration and a University. In Samy, D., Pérez-Fernández, D. and Arenas-García, J. (eds), 1st Workshop on Language Technologies for Government and Public Administration (LT4Gov) Proceedings: LREC 2020 Workshop Language Resources and Evaluation Conference 11–16 May 2020. European Language Resources Association (ELRA), pp. 28–31.

Moczek, N. (2019) Freiwilliges Engagement für Citizen Science-Projekte im Naturschutz: Konstruktion und Validierung eines Skalensystems zur Messung motivationaler und organisationaler Funktionen, 1. Auflage. Lengerich, Pabst Science Publishers.

Nov, O., Arazy, O. and Anderson, D. (2011) Technology-Mediated Citizen Science Participation: A Motivational Model. In, Proceedings of the Fifth International AAAI Conference on Weblogs and Social Media.

OeAD (2022) Become a Citizen Science Award project. https://zentrumfuercitizenscience.at/en/for-researchers/become-a-citizen-science-award-project.

Palacin, V., Gilbert, S., Orchard, S., Eaton, A., Ferrario, M. A. and Happonen, A. (2020) Drivers of Participation in Digital Citizen Science: Case Studies on Järviwiki and Safecast. *Citizen Science: Theory and Practice*, 5, 2020: 10.5334/cstp.290.

Raddick, M. J., Bracey, G., Gay, P. L., Lintott, C. J., Murray, P., Schawinski, K. *et al.* (2010) Galaxy Zoo. Exploring the Motivations of Citizen Science Volunteers. *Astronomy Education Review*, 9, 2010: 10.3847/AER2009036.

Rotman, D., Hammock, J., Preece, J. J., Boston, C. L., Hansen, D. L., Bowser, A. *et al.* (2014) Does motivation in citizen science change with time and culture? In Fussell, S. (ed), Compilation publication of CSCW'14 proceedings & CSCW'14 companion: February 15 - 19, 2014, Baltimore, Maryland, USA. New York, NY, ACM, pp. 229–232.

Rotman, D., Preece, J., Hammock, J., Procita, K., Hansen, D., Parr, C. *et al.* (2012) Dynamic changes in motivation in collaborative citizen-science projects. In Poltrock, S., Simone, C., Grudin, J., Mark, G. and Riedl, J. (eds), the ACM 2012 conference, pp. 217-226.

Schweiz forscht (2021) What's Up, Switzerland? https://www.schweizforscht.ch/projekte/projektarchiv/what-s-up-switzerland.

Tiago, P., Gouveia, M. J., Capinha, C., Santos-Reis, M. and Pereira, H. M. (2017) The influence of motivational factors on the frequency of participation in citizen science activities. *Nature Conservation*, 18, 2017: 10.3897/natureconservation.18.13429.

Zampieri, M., Nakov, P. and Scherrer, Y. (2020) Natural language processing for similar languages, varieties, and dialects: A survey. *Natural Language Engineering*, 26, 2020: 10.1017/S1351324920000492.

7. Language Resource References

IamDiÖ. (2019). Wortgut, https://lex.dioe.at/

Author Index